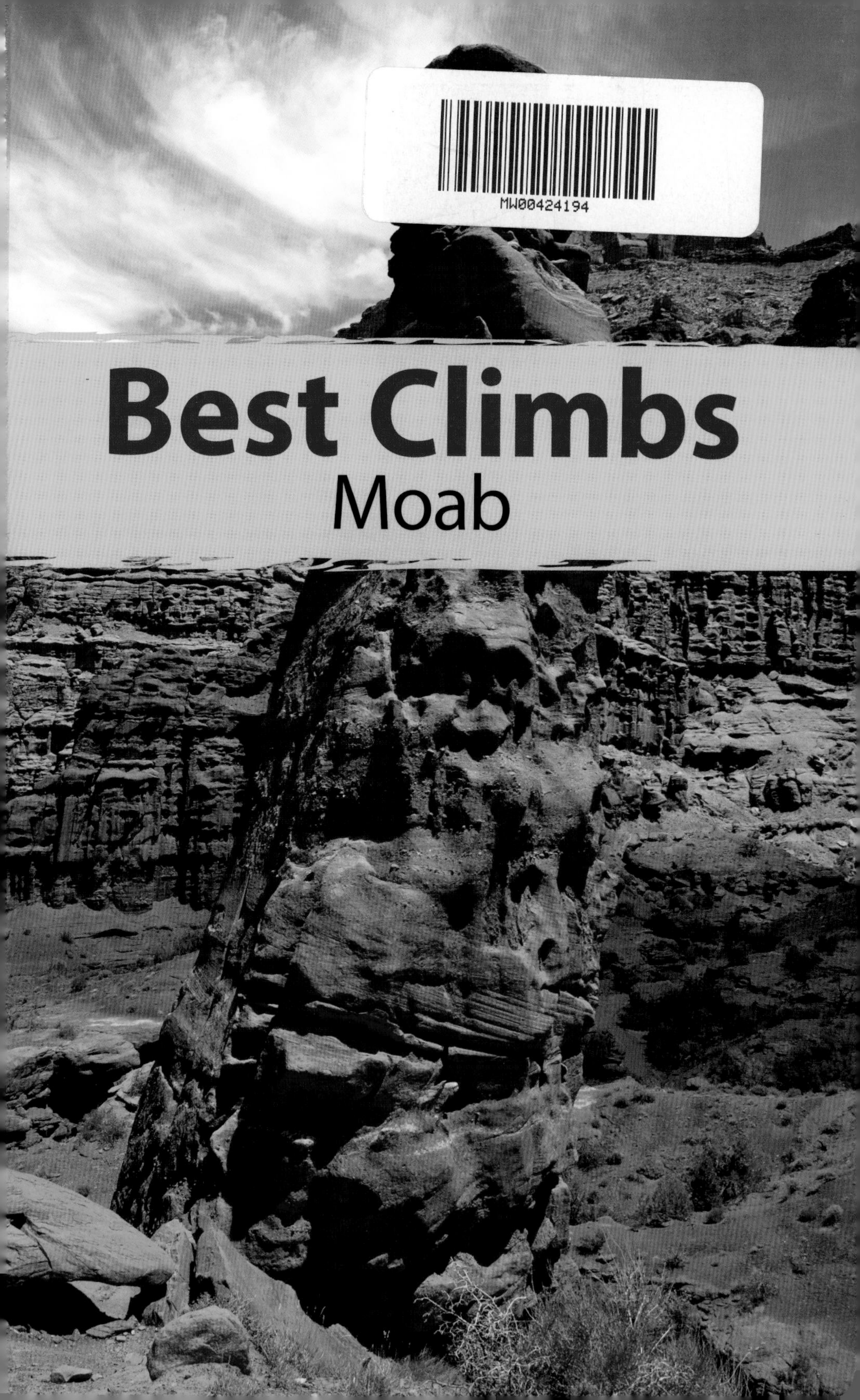

Best Climbs

Moab

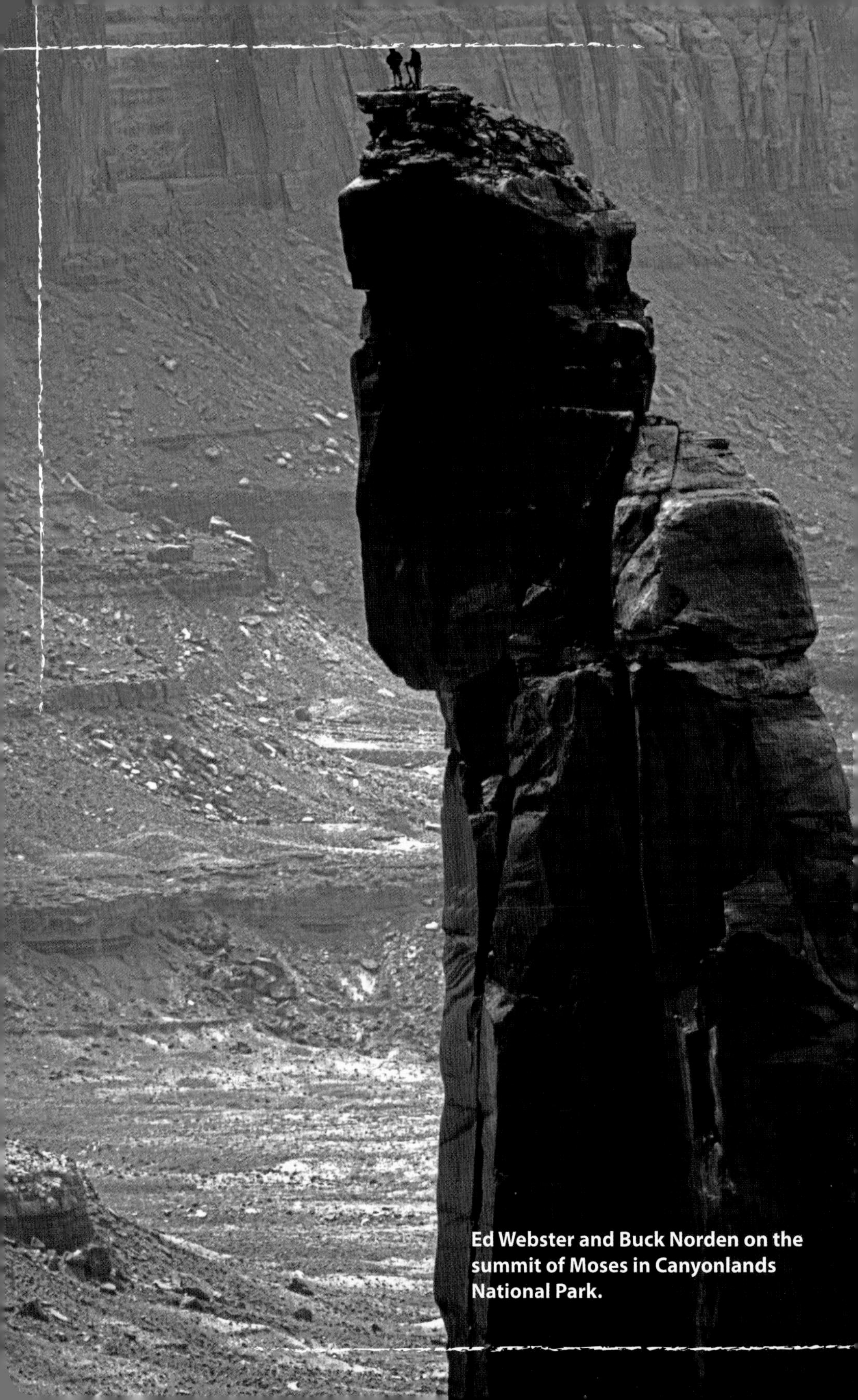

Ed Webster and Buck Norden on the summit of Moses in Canyonlands National Park.

Best Climbs
Moab

Over 140 of the Best Routes in the Area

STEWART M. GREEN

FALCON GUIDES®

GUILFORD, CONNECTICUT
HELENA, MONTANA

AN IMPRINT OF GLOBE PEQUOT PRESS

Dedicated to Layton Kor—the greatest desert climbing pioneer. Layton, thanks for all the great climbs and for your friendship.

FALCONGUIDES®

FalconGuides is an imprint of Globe Pequot Press.
Falcon, FalconGuides, and Outfit Your Mind are registered trademarks of Morris Book Publishing, LLC.

All interior photos by Stewart M. Green unless otherwise noted.

Maps and Topos by Sue Murray © Morris Book Publishing, LLC
Text design: Sheryl P. Kober
Project editor: John Burbidge

Library of Congress Cataloging-in-Publication data is on file.

ISBN 978-0-7627-6058-9

Printed in China

10 9 8 7 6 5 4 3 2 1

WARNING

Climbing is a sport where you may be seriously injured or die. Read this before you use this book.

This guidebook is a compilation of unverified information gathered from many different climbers. The author cannot ensure the accuracy of any of the information in this book, including the topos and route descriptions, the difficulty ratings, and the protection ratings. These may be incorrect or misleading, as ratings of climbing difficulty and danger are always subjective and depend on the physical characteristics (for example, height), experience, technical ability, confidence, and physical fitness of the climber who supplied the rating. Additionally, climbers who achieve first ascents sometimes underrate the difficulty or danger of the climbing route. Therefore, be warned that you must exercise your own judgment on where a climbing route goes, its difficulty, and your ability to safely protect yourself from the risks of rock climbing. Examples of some of these risks are: falling due to technical difficulty or due to natural hazards such as holds breaking, falling rock, climbing equipment dropped by other climbers, hazards of weather and lightning, your own equipment failure, and failure or absence of fixed protection.

You should not depend on any information gleaned from this book for your personal safety; your safety depends on your own good judgment, based on experience and a realistic assessment of your climbing ability. If you have any doubt as to your ability to safely climb a route described in this book, do not attempt it.

The following are some ways to make your use of this book safer:

1. Consultation: You should consult with other climbers about the difficulty and danger of a particular climb prior to attempting it. Most local climbers are glad to give advice on routes in their area; we suggest that you contact locals to confirm ratings and safety of particular routes and to obtain first-hand information about a route chosen from this book.

2. Instruction: Most climbing areas have local climbing instructors and guides available. We recommend that you engage an instructor or guide to learn safety techniques and to become familiar with the routes and hazards of the areas described in this book. Even after you are proficient in climbing safely, occasional use of a guide is a safe way to raise your climbing standard and learn advanced techniques.

3. Fixed Protection: Some of the routes in this book may use bolts and pitons that are permanently placed in the rock. Because of variances in the manner of placement, weathering, metal fatigue, the quality of the metal used, and many other factors, these fixed protection pieces should always be considered suspect and should always be backed up by equipment that you place yourself. Never depend on a single piece of fixed protection for your safety, because you never can tell whether it will hold weight. In some cases, fixed protection may have been removed or is now missing. However, climbers should not always add new pieces of protection unless existing protection is faulty. Existing protection can be tested by an experienced climber and its strength determined. Climbers are strongly encouraged not to add bolts and drilled pitons to a route. They need to climb the route in the style of the first ascent party (or better) or choose a route within their ability—a route to which they do not have to add additional fixed anchors.

Be aware of the following specific potential hazards that could arise in using this book:

1. Incorrect Descriptions of Routes: If you climb a route and you have a doubt as to where it goes, you should not continue unless you are sure that you can go that way safely. Route descriptions and topos in this book could be inaccurate or misleading.

2. Incorrect Difficulty Rating: A route might be more difficult than the rating indicates. Do not be lulled into a false sense of security by the difficulty rating.

3. Incorrect Protection Rating: If you climb a route and you are unable to arrange adequate protection from the risk of falling through the use of fixed pitons or bolts and by placing your own protection devices, do not assume that there is adequate protection available higher just because the route protection rating indicates the route does not have an X or an R rating. Every route is potentially an X (a fall may be deadly), due to the inherent hazards of climbing—including, for example, failure or absence of fixed protection, your own equipment's failure, or improper use of climbing equipment.

There are no warranties, whether expressed or implied, that this guidebook is accurate or that the information contained in it is reliable. There are no warranties of fitness for a particular purpose or that this guide is merchantable. Your use of this book indicates your assumption of the risk that it may contain errors and is an acknowledgment of your own sole responsibility for your climbing safety.

your safety depends on
your own good judgment,
based on experience and
a realistic assessment of
your climbing ability

Moab Overview

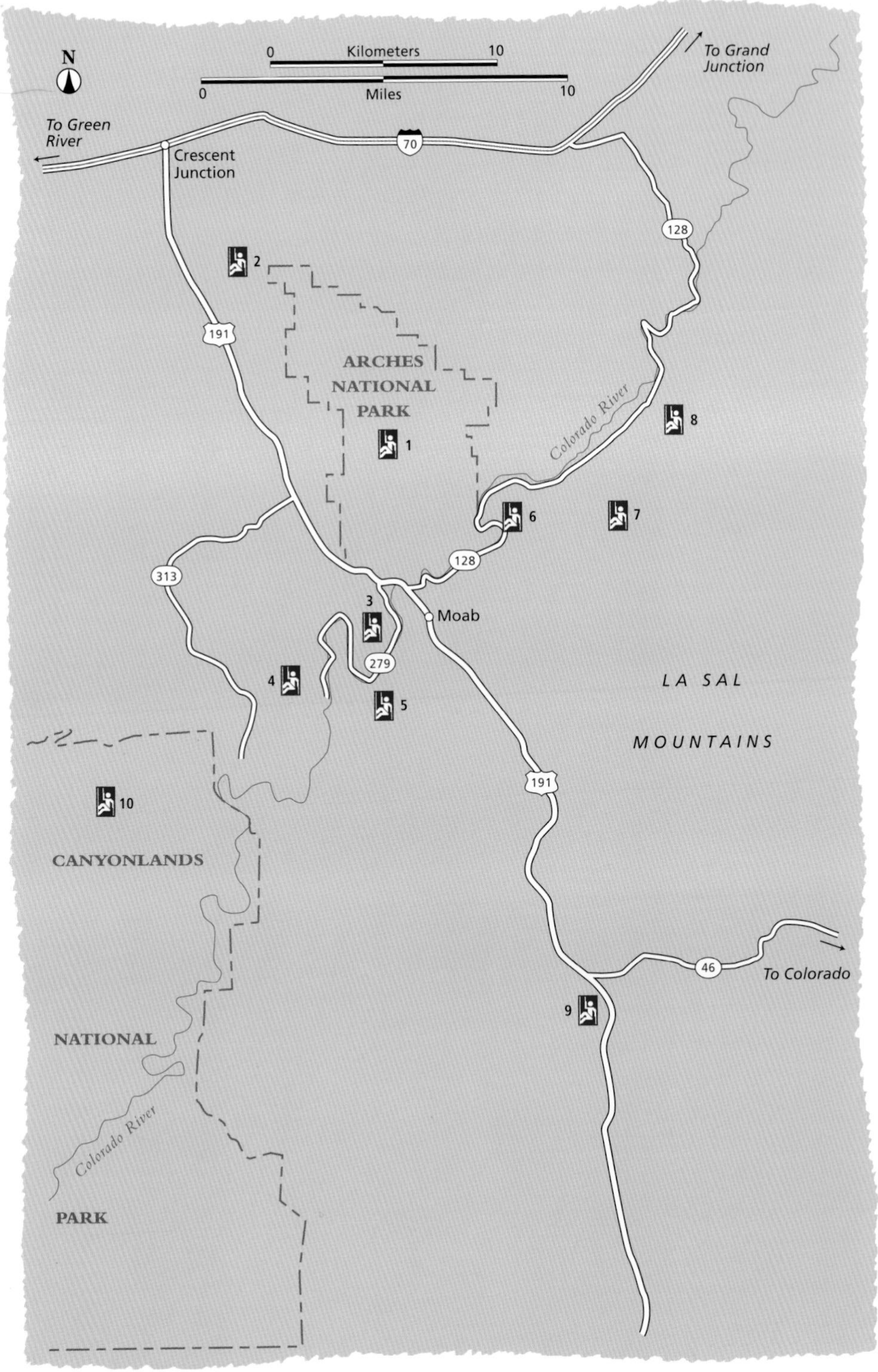

Contents

Introduction

Moab—there's a lot of magic in that name. It conjures up bare-bones landscapes of startling beauty, deep canyons excavated by the Colorado River, distant vistas of peak and plain, long cliff bands of multicolored sandstone, and soaring towers that scrape against the blue sky.

The Moab region, encompassing Arches and Canyonlands National Parks, the Colorado River canyons, and vast uninhabited tracts of slickrock sandstone, is an outdoor paradise for climbers.

It's a savage, remote arena filled with vertical adventures, from easy scrambling routes up Looking Glass Rock and Elephant Butte to hard crack climbs that end on the small summits of frail towers at Castle Valley, Fisher Towers, and the Island in the Sky. Out there, in the sun-baked Moab desert, are bolted sport routes and testy crack climbs at Wall Street, the Ice Cream Parlor, Sunshine Wall, and Maverick Buttress.

Moab's sunny red-rock country offers literally thousands of great routes to climbers of all abilities. *Best Climbs Moab* leads you to the area's very best routes—classic old-school routes on desert towers to bolted climbs up sunny slabs to fun topropes for novice climbers. Out there on the gritty sandstone escarpments, you'll quickly discover the joy of vertical movement, the importance of wild untrammeled places, and the extraordinary sensation of being present in the moment that climbers seek when standing among the rock gods.

Climbing Seasons

While climbing is possible year-round in the desert around Moab, spring and autumn are the best seasons. Spring brings warm days and cool nights, as well as strong winds that can make climbing difficult. Occasional rainstorms occur in spring, sometimes bringing several days of unsettled weather. Summer begins in May with daily highs creeping upward into the 90s. Summer days are generally hot. Moab's average July high temperature is 99 degrees and the average low is 64 degrees. It often climbs above 100 degrees, making climbing impossible except in the early morning. Look for shady cliffs and bring lots of water. May and June are dry, with little rain falling. Thunderstorms often build up on July and August afternoons, but precipitation is localized. Watch out, however, for torrential rain that floods dry washes and cascades off cliffs, as well as lightning, which, like climbers, seeks high places.

Autumn, occurring from mid-September to mid-November, offers ideal climbing weather. Expect clear sunny days with temperatures between 60 and

Brittany Griffith jamming *Boothill* at Maverick Buttress. Photo Andrew Burr

85 degrees. October is the wettest month at Moab. The winter months can be cold and snowy, with an average of 12 inches of snow falling in the average Moab winter. It can also be warm and sunny with daily highs in the 50s and 60s. Plenty of sunny cliffs out of the wind are found, offering pleasant winter climbing.

Climbing Regulations and Etiquette

The Moab climbing areas are all on public lands administered by either the Bureau of Land Management (BLM) or the National Park Service (NPS). While there are few climbing regulations on BLM lands, there are many for Arches and Canyonlands National Parks.

All regulations are intended to protect the unique geological, ecological, and archaeological resources of each national park. These NPS rules include no power drills; no installation of fixed hardware without prior approval except for emergency self-rescue; no dogs in the backcountry; no fires or firewood collecting; no backcountry camping or bivouacking without a permit; no climbing on any named arch or natural bridge labeled on USGS maps; no alteration of the rock including chipping, drilling, or gluing holds; no white chalk; no fixed ropes left in place for more than twenty-four hours; no damage to vegetation or lichen; and no slacklining. All climbing must be hammerless.

When you're climbing Moab's best routes, remember that the canyon country is a fragile environment. Practice a leave-no-trace ethic to protect these wonderful climbing areas and ensure our continued unencumbered access to them.

Follow commonsense rules when climbing in the desert. These include picking up all trash from crags and trails; not altering the rock surface by chipping handholds or removing vegetation from cracks; not driving off-road to reach cliffs; and only camping at existing sites, using existing fire rings and properly disposing of human waste. Some primitive camping areas around Moab, such as the Onion Creek area on BLM land, require all campers to possess and use portable toilets.

It's important to follow existing trails whenever possible to reach climbing areas to avoid damaging cryptobiotic soil, a crunchy black layer that stabilizes the soil and keeps it from eroding. Desert soils are very sensitive to human impact and take years to recover from damage caused by feet, bicycles, and ATVs. Follow drainages or hike on durable surfaces whenever possible.

Lastly, remember that sandstone, the medium we climb on in the Moab desert, is susceptible to damage, especially after rain and snow. Sandstone is porous, and it weakens when it soaks up water. Wet sandstone erodes quickly; flakes become loose and brittle and often break; and holds dissolve into sand. Keep off the sandstone and let it dry completely, usually at least twenty-four hours. Decide if the stone is too wet for climbing by noting if the ground is still damp from rain, the rock still has wet spots, and sand in rock pockets is still moist. If it passes any of these tests, don't climb. Instead go hiking, biking, or hang at a Moab coffee shop and surf the Internet.

Moab, settled in 1878, was named by Mormon settlers in 1880 for a mountainous biblical region east of the Dead Sea. The town became the "Uranium Capital of the World" after Charlie Steen discovered a rich deposit south of town in 1952, setting off a twenty-year mining boom. Now tourist dollars sustain Moab, with visitors flocking to Canyonlands and Arches National Parks and recreating in the surrounding red-rock desert.

Desert Climbing Skills

Moab's best climbs are on different kinds of sandstone. Most towers are composed of Wingate sandstone, a hard compact rock usually split by vertical crack systems. The Arches National Park climbs are on two types of Entrada sandstone, which tends to be soft and rounded. Cutler sandstone, which forms the Fisher Towers, is a coarse conglomerate with few cracks and hanging mud curtains. Wall Street is formed by Navajo sandstone, a thick wind-deposited layer.

Many desert climbs are difficult, especially the Wingate sandstone crack routes on towers. These cracks usually ascend steep faces, have few face edges, and require good crack climbing skills. To climb the big towers like Moses or Castleton, you have to be able to securely jam strenuous cracks and place solid protection from poor stances. Try to place gear at least every body length, since cams can rip out of the soft stone in a leader fall. Protect your hands by taping them with athletic tape.

If you're new to desert sandstone climbing, head to Wall Street. It's easily accessible and has a wide variety of routes including delicate slab and face climbs as well as steep splitter cracks. The Street is a great place to practice and hone your desert climbing skills in a gorgeous riverside setting.

Desert Climbing Rack and Extras

While gear suggestions are included in many route descriptions, what you carry on your climbing rack is up to you. Look at your proposed route and decide what you need to safely protect yourself when you climb. Many tower climbs are complicated, with lots of different-size cracks; make sure you bring enough gear—remember, the sin is never carrying too much gear, but not enough.

For traditional desert routes, you need a full rack of gear. A basic rack should include two to three sets of TCUs and cams to fist-size, one to two sets of wired nuts like Stoppers, ten to twelve slings with extra carabiners, and at least a dozen quickdraws. Some climbs require multiple same-size cams as well as off-width pieces like extra-large cams and Big Bros. Bring two 200-foot (60-meter) ropes for climbing and rappelling, although 165-foot (50-meter) ropes often work fine. Also bring and wear a helmet. Loose rock abounds on the sandstone cliffs and a helmet saves your head.

If you're climbing towers, bring extra webbing and a knife to cut it for replacing old slings on rappel anchors. Webbing wears out quickly in the harsh sun and heat. Bring plenty of water, either in bottles or a hydration pack. Gatorade or other liquids that replace electrolytes are essential for hydration in the heat. Long pants with reinforced knees are great for climbing cracks. Wear sturdy boots or approach shoes for hiking across the spiny desert to your route. Bring a headlamp so you can see if you're benighted on a climb or on the hike out. A small GPS unit can keep you found in the desert, and a cell phone, if you can get service, could be a lifesaver in an emergency.

Climbing Dangers and Safety

Rock climbing is dangerous. That's a fact. The perils of climbing, however, are usually overstated. The risks we take are the ones we choose to take. Everything we do as climbers, including placing gear, setting anchors, tying into the rope, and belaying, is to mitigate the dire effects of gravity and to minimize the danger of climbing. It's up to you to be safe when you're climbing. Be safety conscious and use the buddy system to double-check your partner and yourself.

Redundancy is key to your personal safety. Always back up every important piece of gear with another and use more than one anchor at belay and rappel stations. Your life depends on it. Beginner climbers are most vulnerable to accidents. If you're inexperienced, hire a guide or

> Are there rattlesnakes in the desert? Yes. The midget-faded rattlesnake *(Crotalus viridus concolor)*, a small subspecies of the western rattlesnake, is the only indigenous rattlesnake in the Moab area. They're small, typically 20 to 24 inches long, and a yellowish-cream color with brown blotched patterns. They're also shy, retiring, and rarely seen, living in burrows and rock crevices and being active mostly at night. The snakes produce a neurotoxic venom but rarely bite humans.

Rob Pizem and Mike Brumbaugh cranking the last pitch of *Jah Man* on Sister Superior. PHOTO ANDREW BURR

take lessons. Always use sound judgment when climbing and respect the danger. Don't attempt climbs beyond your ability and experience. Remember that most accidents happen because of climber error.

Objective dangers, as at most climbing areas, abound on the sandstone cliffs and towers around Moab. Watch out for loose rock as you climb or if another party is climbing above. Loose flakes and boulders are commonly found, particularly after freeze-thaw cycles in winter. Wear a helmet to mitigate head injuries when climbing and belaying. Use any fixed gear with caution. Some climbs still have old pitons and bolts, and it's hard to determine how solid they actually are. Weathering and erosion weakens fixed pitons and bolts. Always back up fixed gear with your own. Poison ivy is found along cliff bases, especially at Wall Street. Keep an eye out for shiny leaves and small white berries. Rattlesnakes, while rarely seen, are found at all the climbing venues. Weather can be fickle. Summer thunderstorms move in quickly, so be prepared to bail off your route if necessary. Rain can come down fast and heavy. Watch for lightning on high points like the tops of towers.

Use the following ten tips to stay safe when you're out climbing on the cliffs around Moab:

- Always check your harness.
- Always check knots.
- Always wear a helmet.
- Always check the rope and belay device.
- Always use a long rope.
- Always pay attention.
- Always bring enough gear.
- Always lead with the rope over your leg.
- Always properly clip the rope into carabiners.
- Always use safe and redundant anchors.

To learn more about climbing, including basic skills like creating anchor systems, placing gear, jamming cracks, rappelling, belaying, and tying knots, buy my comprehensive instructional book *KNACK Rock Climbing,* co-authored with Ian Spencer-Green, from Globe Pequot Press.

Map Legend

- Interstate
- US Highway
- State Highway
- Gravel Road
- Unimproved Road
- Trail
- Waterway
- Lake/Reservoir
- Town
- City
- Climbing Area
- Crag/Boulder
- Cliff Edge
- Elevation
- Parking
- Restroom
- Building
- Camping
- Gate
- Point of Interest
- National Forest/
State Park Boundary

Topo Legend

○	Natural gear belay stance
x	Single piece of fixed protection (bolt or piton)
xx	Fixed belay station

Arches National Park

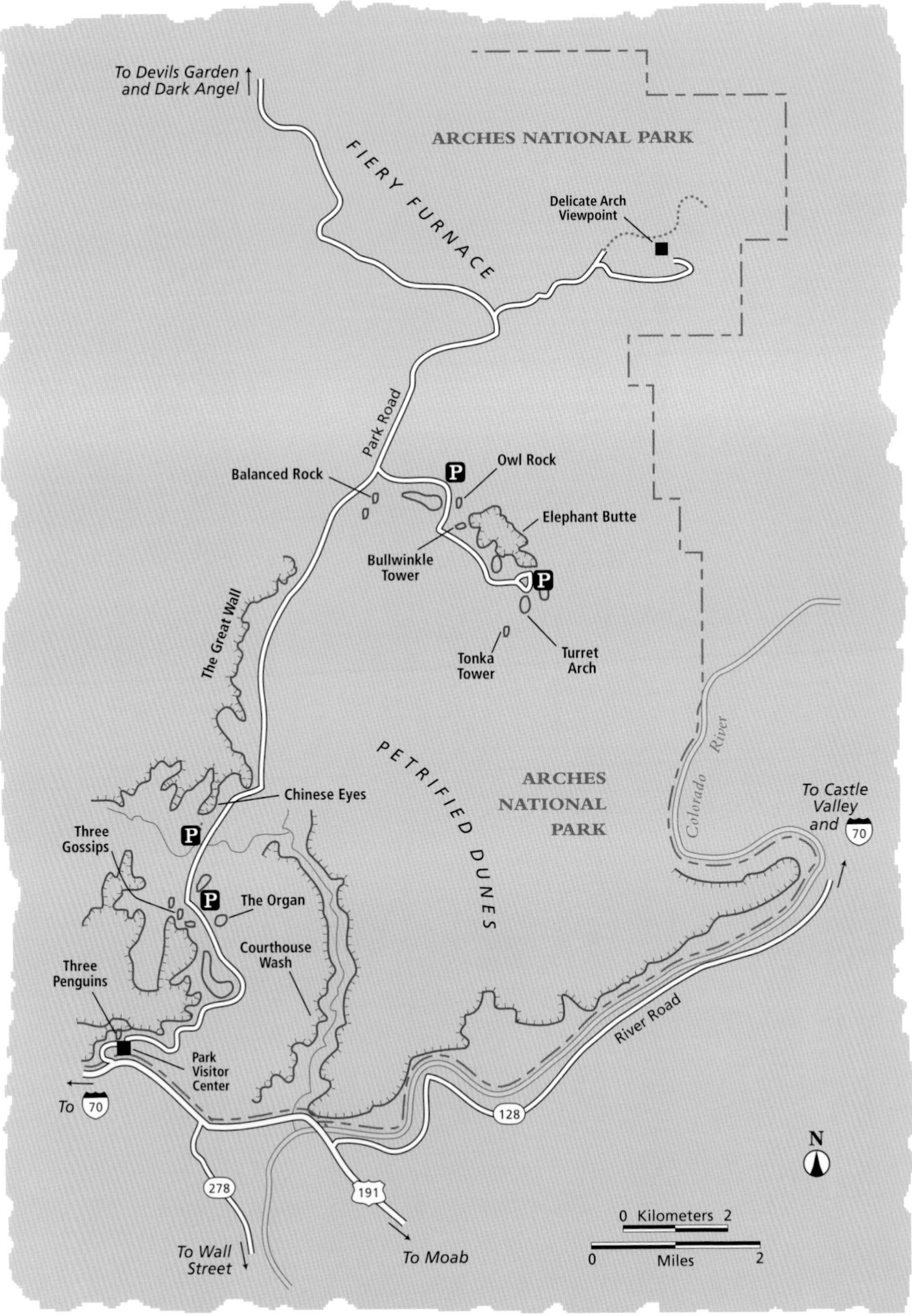

To Devils Garden and Dark Angel
ARCHES NATIONAL PARK
FIERY FURNACE
Delicate Arch Viewpoint
Park Road
Balanced Rock
Owl Rock
Elephant Butte
Bullwinkle Tower
Tonka Tower
Turret Arch
The Great Wall
PETRIFIED DUNES
ARCHES NATIONAL PARK
Colorado River
To Castle Valley and 70
Chinese Eyes
Three Gossips
The Organ
Courthouse Wash
Three Penguins
Park Visitor Center
To 70
River Road
128
278
191
To Wall Street
To Moab
N
0 Kilometers 2
0 Miles 2

1.

Arches National Park

Arches National Park, a 73,234-acre wonderland of sandstone fins, towers, ribs, gargoyles, hoodoos, balanced rocks, and arches northwest of Moab, protects the largest collection of arches in the world. Over 2,000 arches with at least one side 3 or more feet wide have been cataloged by explorers, including 306-foot-long Landscape Arch and Delicate Arch, Utah's state symbol.

While visitors come from around the world to view the arches and scenery, climbers also visit to ascend the park's towers and cliffs. Over a dozen spires up to 300 feet high rise within a ten-minute hike from the park road. The arches and towers are composed of Entrada sandstone, a soft rock deposited as sand dunes during Jurassic times over 160 million years ago. The sandstone at Arches is notoriously sandy, especially after rain or snow. Most routes follow crack systems with only occasional face moves.

Arches National Park has several important climbing regulations to protect the area's unique geological resources. The use of white chalk is banned in the park. Go without chalk or use an earth-tone chalk that matches the sandstone's color. Only rust-colored slings should be used at belay and rappel anchors to minimize visual impact. The use of power drills is prohibited, and no new bolts can be placed without prior permission. Do not climb on or near any arches to avoid damage. Dogs must be leashed at all times and are not allowed on any trails. Dog kennels in Moab can care for your dog while you're climbing. Follow existing paths to the cliffs whenever possible to avoid damaging

Entrada sandstone forms the arches and towers at Arches National Park. The Entrada divides into three separate layers—Dewey Bridge, Slick Rock, and Moab Tongue. Severe wrinkling characterizes the Dewey Bridge layer. It composes Owl Rock, Elephant Butte, Tonka Tower, and the Windows area. The Slick Rock member forms vertical cliffs in the Courthouse Towers area, including the Three Gossips, The Organ, and Three Penguins, as well as Devil's Garden and Fiery Furnace. The Moab Tongue is a thin white caprock atop the Slick Rock member.

Brett Green jamming the upper crack on Owl Rock.

Cryptobiotic soil, composed of a living microscopic organism called *cynaobacteria,* forms a black crust on the ground in the canyon country. Cryptobiotic soil is a valuable part of the ecosystem since it prevents soil erosion by wind and water and retains moisture. This delicate soil is crushed if you step on it. To avoid damaging the crust, follow these guidelines—stay on existing paths, walk single-file, step on durable surfaces like rock or follow washes, and don't camp on it.

fragile cryptobiotic soil. If you have to walk cross-country, avoid the soil and hike on durable rock surfaces or in washes.

Getting there: The main entrance to Arches National Park is 5 miles northwest of Moab on US 191. The paved 24-mile-long park road travels from the visitor center at the entrance to Devil's Garden and the fifty-two-site park campground. All the described climbs begin from this road. Arches National Park is a fee area.

The great American writer Edward Abbey (1927–1989) spent two years as a seasonal ranger in Arches National Monument in the 1950s. *Desert Solitaire,* a memoir detailing his first summer in 1956, burst on the scene in 1968, not only popularizing the canyon country but also changing lives. Ed summarizes his season in the wilderness in the last chapter: "The finest quality of this stone, these plants and animals, this desert landscape is the indifference to our presence, our absence, our coming, our staying or our going. Whether we live or die is a matter of absolutely no concern whatsoever to the desert."

The Three Penguins

The Three Penguins

The 140-foot-high Three Penguins tower above the park road as it loops up Headquarters Hill just past the visitor center. The *Right Chimney* route is one of Arches' best climbs with good stone and superb jamming.

Approach: From the park visitor center, drive up the road to a pull-out at 0.9 mile (GPS N 38.37.177 / W 109.36.917). Park and scramble up a loose mudstone gully to a horizontal ledge system that the Penguins sit on. Follow the ledge to the base of the east face above the road.

1. Right Chimney (5.10c) Excellent route up an obvious right-facing dihedral. **Pitch 1:** Jam a perfect crack that widens from hands to fists (5.10c) to a 3-bolt ledge belay. 80 feet. **Pitch 2:** Continue up the steep crack—hands to fists to off-width (5.10a). Above, face climb to the summit of the center Penguin. **Descent:** Double-rope, 140-foot rappel from a 3-bolt anchor down the route. **Rack:** Two sets of Friends with extra #2.5s to #4s, one #4 Camalot, and large Stoppers for the start.

California climbers Steve Roper and Allen Steck made the first ascent of The Three Gossips in October 1970. Roper, who made the 1963 third ascent of Castleton, let Steck, a sandstone virgin, do the first pitch up the *West Face* route. "He pounded pins up the long initial crack for hours, it seemed," Roper later wrote. "Once in a while he would yell down: 'I wonder if this one's any good?' I would yell back: 'It's up to you, man, but, hell, didn't you hear it ring?' Meanwhile I braced myself to catch a fall, for sandstone was not granite, and a ring in the one was not the same as a ring in the other." When Roper cleaned the pitch, none of the pitons pulled out although they "shifted and creaked." At the top, Steck led the final pitch, which Roper noted was "a bold end to our insignificant first ascent."

The Three Gossips

The Three Gossips, one of the most impressive formations in the park's Courthouse Towers section, is a spectacular trio of blocky summits towering 300 feet above a rounded slickrock base. The Gossips rise south of the park road and west of the Park Avenue trail. The *West Face,* the formation's best climb, ascends the west face of the Gossips opposite the road.

Approach: Reach the Three Gossips by driving 3.5 miles from the park entrance to the Courthouse Towers/ Park Avenue parking area west of The Organ on the north side of the road

(GPS N 38.38.214 / W 109.36.006). Park and walk a quarter mile west on the road shoulder to a dry wash on the left. Follow the wash south to sandy slopes below the formation. Continue up a climber's path to the slickrock slabs below the west face. Avoid walking on and damaging the fragile cryptobiotic soil by staying in the wash and following existing trails.

2. West Face (II 5.11c or 5.9 C1) Excellent and continuous route up a crack system on the left side of the face to the shoulder right of the North Gossip. The hard parts are easily clean-aided. **Pitch 1:** Do an awkward mantle (5.9) onto a shelf. Jam a thin hand and hand crack (5.9+) up a flared dihedral until it widens. Continue up the off-width crack (5.10+) over a roof to a good belay ledge with 3 bolts. **Pitch 2:** Jam a thin hand crack (5.10-) past a block on the right. Continue up an off-width crack (5.10) for another 50 feet. Stem left to a parallel crack system and begin the route's crux. Jam and stem up the thin finger crack and seam into a tight corner (5.11b/c). Finish up a squeeze chimney (5.7). Belay from a 3-bolt anchor on a ledge below the summit block. **Pitch 3:** Climb a sandy slab (5.7) up right to a hidden 4-foot-wide chimney (5.5) that splits the summit block. Climb the unprotected chimney (5.5) to the summit. **Descent:** Three rappels down the route. **Rappel 1:** Summit to anchors on the saddle atop pitch 2 (50 feet). **Rappel 2:** 110-foot rappel (two ropes) to pitch 1's anchors. **Rappel 3:** 120-foot rappel to the base. Be careful pulling ropes—they can jam. **Rack:** Sets of Stoppers and TCUs, two sets of cams, a couple larger pieces, and two ropes. If you aid, bring extra 2- to 3-inch pieces.

The Three Gossips

The Great Wall

The Great Wall

The Great Wall is a tall sandstone escarpment that forms an unbroken cliff for almost 4 miles from the north side of Courthouse Wash to a collection of small pinnacles. Only a handful of climbs are found on the wall. *Chinese Eyes,* named for two large eye-shaped holes above the route, is the best climb here.

Approach: Drive 4.6 miles north from the visitor center on the park road and park at the Courthouse Wash pullout on the left side of the road just past Courthouse Wash Bridge or at a pullout farther north on the west side of the road (GPS N 38.39.237 / W 109.35.651). Locate the route to the northwest and follow a path to the base of the obvious block. Avoid hiking on cryptobiotic soil.

3. Chinese Eyes (5.9+) Fun but sandy route up a crack in a left-facing corner on the south end of The Great Wall. Jam the center crack system (fingers and hands to off-width) up the left-facing corner to a 2-bolt anchor. 70 feet. **Descent:** Lower or rappel from bolt anchors. **Rack:** Double sets of cams from 1 to 3.5 inches and a #5 Camalot.

Off Balanced Rock

Off Balanced Rock is a blocky formation north of Balanced Rock and south of the intersection of the park road and the Windows road. The *North Chimney* route, climbing an

Off Balanced Rock

obvious crack and chimney system on the shady north side, is popular and fun. It's a sandbag at its traditional 5.7 grade. The first 30 feet of the second pitch is strenuous, awkward, and unprotected unless you have Big Bros. Some serious leader falls and accidents have occurred on this pitch. Use caution.

Approach: From the visitor center, drive 9.3 miles on the park road to a right (east) turn onto the signed Windows road. Park just east of the intersection at a gravel pullout on the right (south) side of the road (GPS N 38.42.212 / W 109.33.754). Hike south for five minutes to the base of the north face. Follow drainages to minimize damage to cryptobiotic soil.

4. North Chimney (5.8 R) Start below a crack behind a big boulder (GPS N 38.42.121 / W 109.33.800). **Pitch 1:** Jam a hand crack (5.6), then climb right along a crack. Face climb up right along a short hand crack to a belay ledge with three bolts. **Pitch 2:** Thrutch up the awkward, unprotected off-width crack above the belay (5.8 R) or layback it (5.7 R) to another off-width section (5.8 R). Protect the off-width with Big Bros. After 40 feet, move into a chimney. Work horizontally right in the back and knee chimney for 50 feet to a vertical crack on the left wall. Climb the widening chimney (5.7), placing gear in the crack, to a 3-bolt/piton anchor below the summit. Scramble onto

Owl Rock

the summit. **Descent:** Two single-rope rappels with a 200-foot (60-meter) rope down the route or a double-rope 160-foot rappel to the ground. **Rack:** Double sets of Camalots to #3 and two ropes or a 200-foot (60-meter) rope.

Owl Rock

Owl Rock, a classic roadside spire, offers moderate climbing up a steep crack system. The 100-foot-high tower climb is popular, and the sandstone is better than it looks. Owl Rock is one of the easiest towers in the Moab area and is Arches' most popular route.

Approach: From the visitor center, follow the park road north for 9.3 miles to the signed Windows road. Turn right (east) on the Windows road and drive 1.1 miles to the Garden of Eden Overlook parking area on the left (GPS N 38.41.873 / W 109.33.007). Owl Rock is the obvious tower a couple hundred feet southeast of the parking lot. Hike to the base of a crack on the west face.

5. Owl Rock (5.8) Excellent climbing to a small summit. Begin below a crack splitting the west face (GPS N 38.41.833 / W 109.32.959). Swing up the crack with jugs, horns, and knobs to a ledge with a 3-bolt anchor about 10 feet below the summit. Scramble up easy rock to the top, then downclimb back to the anchor. **Descent:** Rappel 95 feet. **Rack:** Set of cams including a 4-inch piece, extra slings. Large Hexentric nuts work well.

Elephant Butte

Elephant Butte, the highest point in Arches National Park at 5,653 feet, is a large sandstone butte surrounded by fins, towers, and arches. Its spacious summit is reached by an interesting, circuitous route that winds through narrow canyons, scrambles up slickrock slabs, and includes a couple of rappels. On your first trip up the Elephant, plan to get lost, use routefinding skills, and have a grand adventure. The route, more of a mountaineering excursion than a rock climb, is mostly third-class scrambling with only one short step of technical climbing. If you're not used to slab climbing, use a rope and rock shoes on the unprotected slickrock sections.

Approach: Drive north from the park entrance and visitor center for 9.3 miles to the signed Windows road on the right. Turn right (east) on the Windows road and drive 1.1 miles to the Garden of Eden Overlook parking area on the left (GPS N 38.41.873 / W 109.33.007). Owl Rock is the obvious spire near the parking area. Elephant Butte is the complex formation east of Owl Rock.

Finding the start of the route is the first routefinding dilemma. From the parking area, hike south around Owl Rock to the drainage between it and Bullwinkle Tower. Hike east up the drainage between two fins. The left fin has a small arch on its east end. Straight ahead are three wide fins divided by two canyons. The route begins at the entrance to the left (north) canyon, its mouth choked with big boulders and rubble (GPS N 38.41.795 / W 109.32.771).

6. West Fins (5.3) Great mountaineering adventure. Follow the above directions to the mouth of the left canyon to start. Scramble over boulders and rubble into the narrow canyon and hike until it narrows and ends in a chimney. Climb a crack and ramp (3rd class) on the right side to a ledge, then drop into a shallow gash to the left. Climb a short chimney to the upper canyon. Hike up the sandy canyon for a few hundred feet to the first side canyon on the right. Climb a short slab into the slickrock canyon and follow it south, passing through a narrow slot to a ledge below a step. Climb the step on either the left or right (5.3), then scramble to a notch and belay. Climb down the south side of the notch and traverse an exposed ledge left to a 5-bolt rappel anchor. Rappel 85 feet into a stone canyon, then downclimb a short groove to an open bowl. Go left and clamber over big boulders, then climb a couple hundred feet up sandstone slabs (3rd class) to a steep cliff band. Climb right below the band to its far right side and work up an easy break to a wide terrace. Cross the terrace and locate a short chimney on the right side of the upper cliff band. Climb the chimney (3rd class) and then hike northeast to the summit cairn and register. **Descent:** The descent route does not reverse the ascent route. Downclimb back to the top of the slabs. Descend the left slab (3rd class) for a couple hundred feet to a small pinnacle. Scramble down a slickrock canyon below the pinnacle. The canyon narrows, reaches a water-filled pothole, and ends at an overhanging drop-off with a 3-piton anchor. Make a free 75-foot rappel to the cliff base. Coil your rope and hike down the canyon below to the end of a long fin. Turn right and hike cross-country over a couple drainages back to Owl Rock and the parking area. **Rack:** Slings, 165-foot (50-meter) rope, and extra webbing if rappel anchors need replacing.

Elephant Butte

Stewart Green squeezes up a chimney on Bullwinkle Tower in Arches National Park.
PHOTO DENNIS JUMP

Bullwinkle Tower

Bullwinkle Tower, a 90-foot-high spire south of Owl Rock, offers fun climbing, a nice summit, and easy access. It's easily recognized from the Windows road by a chimney that splits the tower into two halves.

Approach: From the visitor center, follow the park road north for 9.3 miles to the signed Windows road. Turn right (east) on the Windows road and drive 1.1 miles to the Garden of Eden Overlook parking area on the left (GPS N 38.41.873 / W 109.33.007). Owl Rock is southeast of the parking lot. Bullwinkle Tower is just beyond Owl Rock. Hike south to the slabs on the southwest side of the tower. Alternatively, drive the Windows road until it ends. Follow the loop and backtrack until you're directly south of Bullwinkle. Park on the road's wide shoulder south of the tower. Hike north on slabs around the left side of a low formation to the base of the tower.

7. West Chimney (5.6) Start on the slabs on the southwest side of the tower (GPS N 38.41.715 / W 109.32.899). Scramble up an easy slab to a bulge and pull past on the left (5.6), then move right to the base of a crack. Jam the off-width crack, then work up the chimney above (5.5) to a 3-bolt anchor. Scramble onto the higher north summit. Don't toprope this route with a slingshot belay from the base—your rope could pull off loose blocks near the top. **Descent:** Rappel 90 feet. **Rack:** Bring a #4.5 Camalot, four or five slings, and a 200-foot (60-meter) rope.

Bullwinkle Tower

Tonka Tower

Tonka Tower

Tonka Tower, an isolated 150-foot-high tower southwest of Turret Arch, is a good adventure climb with an exposed summit, strange climbing, and a wild rappel. It's just south of the popular Windows area, so the first part of the approach hike teems with tourists. If you hike out to the tower on busy weekends, be prepared to explain to a ranger your knowledge of cryptobiotic soils and why you won't walk on them. The soil, which forms a hardened surface layer, stabilizes sand and allows plants to grow. Whenever hiking in canyon country, follow washes, durable rock surfaces, and existing paths to avoid damaging the soil.

Approach: Drive 9.3 miles north on the park road from the visitor center and turn right (east) onto the Windows road. Continue for 2.4 miles to a large parking area at the end of the road. Follow the Windows trail to the east side of Turret Arch. Turn south and hike along slickrock slabs below the arch and the formation south of it before heading southwest across slickrock and sandy washes to the group of towers farthest south. Tonka Tower is the middle of three towers (GPS N 38.41.228 / W 109.32.200).

8. Tonka Tower (5.8 A0) Good climbing up a grungy-looking crack system on the left side of the west face. **Pitch 1:** Scramble up easy rock and enter a chimney. Climb to a ledge. Clip a drilled angle on a headwall above and pull (A0) to a spacious ledge with a bolted belay. 120 feet. **Pitch 2:** This lead clips a short bolt ladder (A0) to an exciting mantle (5.8) onto the rounded summit. **Descent:** Double-rope 150-foot rappel down the east face from three drilled angles. Be careful not to get the rope stuck. **Rack:** Set of cams, large Stoppers, slings, and two ropes.

Sunshine Wall

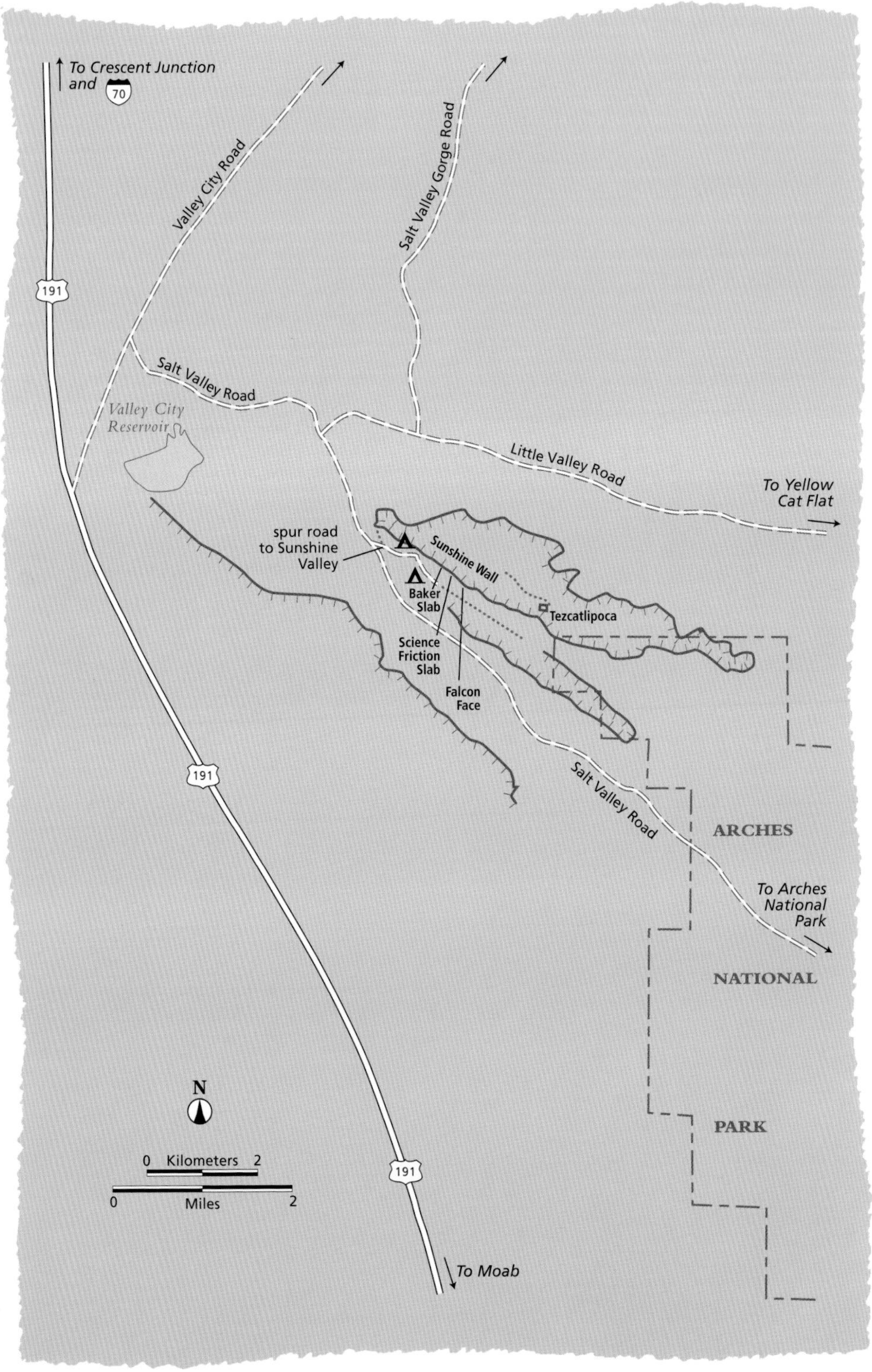
To Crescent Junction
and
70
Valley City Road
Salt Valley Gorge Road
191
Salt Valley Road
Valley City
Reservoir
Little Valley Road
To Yellow
Cat Flat
spur road
to Sunshine
Valley
Sunshine Wall
Baker
Slab
Tezcatlipoca
Science
Friction
Slab
Falcon
Face
191
Salt Valley Road
ARCHES
To Arches
National
Park
NATIONAL
N
PARK
0 Kilometers 2
191
0 Miles 2
To Moab

2.

Sunshine Wall

Sunshine Wall is a southwest-facing Wingate sandstone cliff in the northern end of Salt Valley and a few miles north of Arches National Park. The long cliff, easily accessed from US 191 and I-70, offers lots of good bolted slab routes in a beautiful desert setting. It's a particularly good climbing venue during the cooler months since it receives lots of sunshine. Access, however, is troublesome after rain and snow because the dirt roads to the cliff can become impassable with mud. The wall is on BLM public land and has no current restrictions. Free camping is found below the base of the wall. Bring water and camp at existing sites. Most of the routes are over 100 feet long. Use a 70-meter rope or two ropes to rappel from anchors.

Getting there: Drive south from I-70 on US 191 for 4.2 miles or 27 miles north on US 191 from Moab and turn east on an unmarked dirt road (Valley City Road) between mile markers 152 and 153 (GPS N 38.52.37.09 / W 109.48.44.80).

Bump across railroad tracks and follow the road for 1.2 miles to a right turn on Salt Valley Road just past a white bridge. Drive southeast to another road junction, then bear right and head southeast down upper Salt Valley toward Arches National Park. The hogback with Sunshine Wall rises above the road. Drive 1.4 miles to a road that branches left to the obvious cliffs. Follow this rough road to the cliff and campsites. One camping area is to the left in a wide alcove (GPS N 38.51.42.45 / W 109.44.40.75) and another is to the right by a large boulder with a naked lady petroglyph carved by a cowboy (GPS N 38.51.36.36 / W 109.44.33.78). Routes are described from left to right.

Baker Slab

Baker Slab, named for the late Mike Baker, who established most of the routes here, is the left slab on the main wall. It's characterized by slashing seam cracks. All the routes begin from a ledge with a belay bolt below the slab. Reach the ledge by hiking up through a boulder field and then scrambling up left onto the ledge. Alternatively, a direct start (5.8) with one bolt climbs below the belay bolt. (GPS N 38.51.38 / W 109.44.33).

Descent: Rappel or lower off all routes from bolt anchors.

Baker Slab

1. Unknown (5.9+) On the left side. Climb over boulders to the base of a thin left-facing corner. Edge and smear up the corner past bolts to a 2-bolt anchor.

2. Mosquito Coast (5.8 R) Pull over a short headwall, then smear up the slab above to easier climbing. 4 pitons and bolts to 2-bolt anchor.

3. Learning Curve (5.7) Start just left of the belay bolt. Clip a bolt and climb an incipient crack up the slab until it ends, then step right and follow another crack. 5 bolts to 2-bolt anchor.

4. Love Hurts (5.9) Right of the belay bolt. Work up right along an angling seam to a short crux, then smear up left on easier rock to anchors. 8 bolts and pitons to 2-bolt anchor.

5. Lesson in Braille (5.10c) Excellent slab climb. Start on the far right side of the ledge at some boulders. Friction up right on bumps and smears and finish just right of a sharp arête. 9 bolts to 2-bolt anchor.

Science Friction Slab

Science Friction Slab

The following three routes ascend a beautiful slab right of Baker Slab. Access it from the valley floor by scrambling through a boulder field or traverse east from Baker Slab along the cliff base. (GPS N 38.51.36 / W 109.44.29). **Descent:** Rappel or lower off all routes from bolt anchors.

6. Melanoma Shuffle (5.8+) Excellent. Climb the left side of the slab using bumps, knobs, and smears to anchors. 140 feet. 9 bolts to 2-bolt anchor.

7. Science Friction (5.9+) Fun route up the middle. Start at the slab's low point and smear directly up to a crux. Continue to some holes and finish up a runout seam crack to anchors. 10 bolts/pitons to 2-bolt anchor.

8. Unknown (5.11) Climb edges up a maroon face. Pull past an overlap and smear up the slab above to anchors on the headwall. 10 bolts to 2-bolt anchor.

Falcon Face

Falcon Face

The next big slab right of Science Friction Slab. Access it by hiking up the valley past the first slabs, then following a rough path through boulders to the cliff base. A falcon sometimes nests above the slab. (GPS N 38.51.35 / W 109.44.26). **Descent:** Rappel or lower off all routes from bolt anchors.

9. Walking on Sunshine (5.10d) Superb but thin climb. Expect serious smearing. Start right of a sandy corner. Climb directly to the third bolt, then work up right to a tenuous mantle. Hard smearing above leads to the upper friction slab. 10 bolts to 2-bolt anchor.

10. Brainiac (5.12- or 5.10a A0) Excellent. Begin just right of *Walking on Sunshine.* A hard mantle and thin moves (5.12- or A0) to bolt 2. Continue with sustained edge and friction moves to a thin arch and the final upper slab. 10 bolts to 2-bolt anchor.

Tezcatlipoca

Tezcatlipoca, named for the Aztec god of the night sky, is a fun 50-foot-high spire in a remote and beautiful setting in a maze of slickrock canyons above the Sunshine Wall. It's reached by an hour-long hike up slickrock benches—a long hike to a short climb.

Approach: Start the approach hike at the far left (west) end of the long Sunshine Wall hogback (GPS N 38.86.461 / W 109.74.93). Hike

Tezcatlipoca

southeast on a bench, passing above a short varnished slab with toprope anchors. Continue up the bench, steadily gaining elevation until you're above the Sunshine Wall routes. Eventually the bench ends at cliffs to the right. Scramble over a high point and descend toward a short stubby pinnacle. Turn right here and hike toward a maze of shallow sandstone canyons. Keep a careful eye out to locate Tezcatlipoca, a short spire perched on a slickrock ridge (GPS N 38.51.18 / W 109.43.49). Start the route on the right side of the northeast face. Allow about an hour of hiking and plan on spending some time finding the tower.

11. Tezcatlipoca (5.7) Start on a sloping slab below a short crack. Climb the short, wide crack to a notch, then step left and smear to a piton. Make a tricky move (5.7) and mantle onto the flat summit and a belay/rappel anchor. **Descent:** Rappel 50 feet. **Rack:** Medium and large Camalots.

The late Mike Baker rope-soloed the first ascent of Tezcatlipoca by moonlight in June 1998. He named it for the Aztec god of the night sky, hurricanes, discord, temptation, sorcery, and war. Tezcatlipoca, translated from Nuhuatl as "Lord of the Smoking Mirror," was a black magician who wore a black mirror on his chest, which allowed him to see the deeds of humans and to kill enemies.

Brian Shelton waits while Bill Springer rappels off *Tezcatlipoca* above the Sunshine Wall.

Wall Street

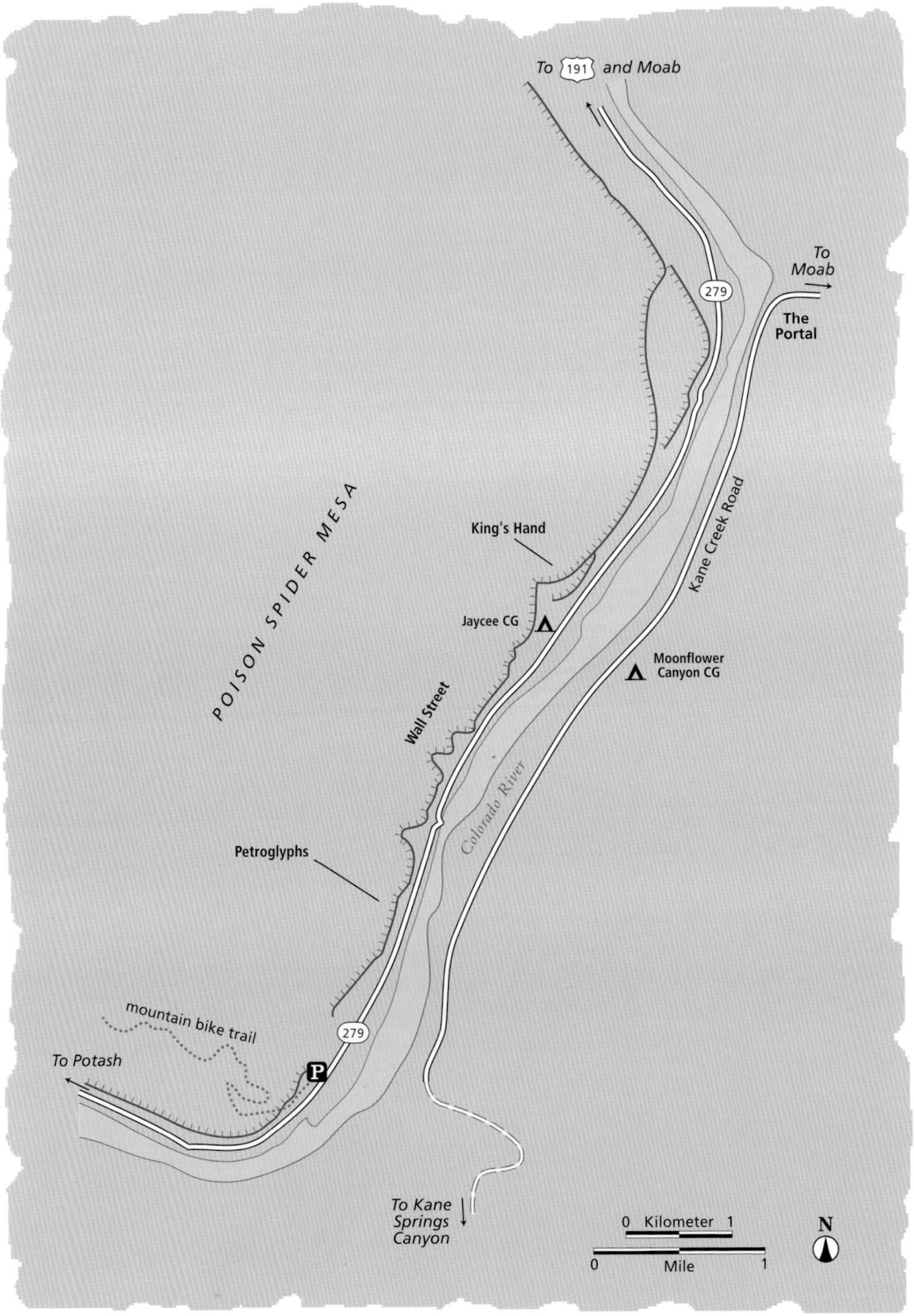

To 191 and Moab
To Moab
279
The Portal
Kane Creek Road
King's Hand
Jaycee CG
Moonflower Canyon CG
POISON SPIDER MESA
Wall Street
Colorado River
Petroglyphs
mountain bike trail
279
To Potash
P
To Kane Springs Canyon
0 Kilometer 1
0 Mile 1
N

3.

Wall Street

Wall Street, the most popular climbing area near Moab, is a towering 500-foot-high cliff that looms above the Colorado River and UT 279. The highway, called the Potash Road, is sandwiched between the cliffs and the river. The cliff, composed of Navajo sandstone, is easily accessed from numerous pullouts below the routes. Access time from car to cliff is usually less than a minute, making Wall Street the ultimate roadside crag.

Wall Street offers a different climbing experience than other Moab area cliffs. Instead of jamming cracks like at Indian Creek or Maverick Buttress, most of Wall Street's routes are face climbing adventures that utilize delicate friction smears, flakes, dimples, and occasional huecos and pockets. Wall Street, however, does offer a selection of excellent crack climbs.

With more than one hundred routes, Wall Street presents a huge variety of accessible routes for climbers, from easy beginner slabs to desperate face climbing test-pieces. Most of the lines are single-pitch, bolt-protected sport routes that range in difficulty from 5.4 to 5.12, with the majority falling in the popular 5.10 category.

While there are no climbing restrictions at Wall Street, follow some commonsense rules to stay safe. Remember that Potash Road is a state highway and can have a lot of traffic, particularly big trucks coming from the Potash Mine to the south. They drive fast, they have the right-of-way, and they don't like to slow down! Park well off the pavement in pullouts and keep your rope, equipment, dog, and yourself off the asphalt. Don't stop on the highway to scope out climbs.

Many Wall Street routes were put up on lead, so the first bolt is often high. Use a stick-clip or climb within your ability to avoid ground falls. Never rely on a single anchor to lower or rappel. Fixed protection can be untrustworthy in sandstone. Rappel whenever possible to avoid damaging the soft rock by lowering. Watch out for poison sumac below many climbs in summer. Keep your rope and yourself out of it to avoid irritating rashes. Lastly, don't climb by the Anasazi petroglyphs at the south end of Wall Street—it's against the law.

Getting there: Wall Street is a ten-minute drive southwest of Moab. Drive a couple miles west from Moab

Jimmie Dunn and Betsy McKittrick make Wall Street the ultimate roadside crag.

PHOTO COURTESY JIMMIE DUNN

On the far south end of Wall Street is one of the best panels of Native American petroglyphs in the Moab area. Park at the INDIAN WRITINGS sign. Across the highway stretches a marvelous gallery of petroglyphs pecked into the rock surface by the ancient ones. These Indians, part of the Fremont Culture, created anthropomorphic figures, bighorn sheep, deer, hunters, and shield figures here between 1300 AD and 600 AD. The petroglyphs are well above ground level since soil below the cliff was moved in highway construction. Boulders with dinosaur tracks are found just down the road at Poison Spider Trailhead.

on US 191 (1.3 miles west of the Colorado River Bridge), to a left (south) turn on UT 279/Potash Road. This turn is just east of the Arches National Park entrance. Drive south on UT 279 for 2 miles and enter The Portal, where the Colorado River leaves Spanish Valley and enters a canyon. After a couple more miles the highway reaches Wall Street, a long band of cliffs alongside the road. Use pullouts along the highway to park. Routes are listed from right to left when facing the cliff.

Key mileages to cliff sectors are: *Seibernetics* area 4.4 miles, the School Room 4.5 miles, *Bad Moki Roof/Flakes of Wrath* 4.6 miles, *Sedan Delivery* and a large parking area 4.7 miles, *Nervous in Suburbia* 4.8 miles, *Static Cling* and a large parking area 4.9 miles, and *Steel Your Face* and the *Slabs* 5.0 miles. A petroglyph panel marks the southern end of Wall Street.

The first routes are on the first buttress that meets the road at 4.4 miles. Wall Street begins at GPS N 38.32.774 / W 109.35.961. **Descent:** Rappel or lower from all routes.

Wall Street

1. Scratch and Sniff (5.11 R) Friction climb up a slab right of an obvious corner. 80 feet. 2 bolts to 2-bolt anchor. Traverse right from *Seibernetics*'s anchors to set up a toprope.

2. Seibernetics (5.8+) Fun climb. Stem, smear, and jam up a seam and crack in an obvious right-facing corner. Two drilled angles protect the middle. **Rack:** Set of Friends or Camalots, TCUs, and Stoppers. (GPS N 38.33.118 / W 109.35.727)

3. Unemployment Line (5.10+) Start left of *Seibernetics*. Work up a leaning right-facing corner to a small ledge with a 2-bolt anchor. A second pitch smears the slab above past three bolts to a 3-bolt anchor.

The next routes are on the cliff section past a deep gully and some hackberry trees. **Descent:** Rappel or lower from all routes.

The Potash Road, built in 1960, accesses North America's largest potash deposit. Potash, used as a water softener and fertilizer, is extracted by solution mining. Colorado River water pumps through the Potash Mine's 340 miles of shafts and drifts, creating a solution of potash and salts that is then pumped into settling ponds, where the water evaporates. Later it's processed, bagged, and shipped by truck and railroad. Watch out for speeding potash trucks along Wall Street!

Wall Street

4. Seam as It Ever Was (5.11b/c) Left of a gully crack. Crux climbing up a fingertip seam leads to a flare and a bulge. 85 feet. 1 bolt and 2 anchors. **Rack:** Small Stoppers, RPs, and TCUs (bring #0s).

5. Rude Old Men (5.12) Sustained friction and edging to anchors in a horizontal seam. 60 feet. 6 pitons/bolts to 2-bolt anchor.

The next routes are on a black varnished wall just left of *Rude Old Men.* **Descent:** Rappel or lower from all routes.

6. Faith Flake (5.11a) A hackberry tree hides the start. Climb past the "faith flake" and up left in a narrow right-facing corner. 3 pitons to 2-bolt anchor. 60 feet. **Rack:** #.75 TCU for crack above the last piton.

7. El Face-o Diablo (5.11d) Tricky, thin, and crimpy. Climb flakes and edges up a black varnished wall. 3 bolts to 3-bolt anchor.

8. El Cracko Diablo (5.10a) Excellent. Finger jam up a flared V-slot to a flake with hand cracks on either side to an upper crux. Step right to 3-bolt anchor. **Rack:** Friends from #1 to #3 and a set of TCUs.

The next cliff section is a long slab a couple hundred feet south of the above routes. **Descent:** Rappel or lower from all routes.

Wall Street

Wall Street

9. School Room Topropes (5.4 to 5.10) Numerous toprope routes are on the slabs above a large pullout. Many sets of bolt anchors are below the bench above the cliff. Most routes are between 5.5 and 5.7, making them popular with groups and beginners. Routes on the right side are steeper and harder. Scramble up easy rock (4th class) above a tree on the far left side to access the anchors. (GPS N 38.33.068 / W 109.35.777)

The next four routes are on a small buttress left of the School Room slabs. **Descent:** Rappel or lower from all routes.

10. Doctor Strange Flake (5.10) Tricky climbing up the right side of the buttress. 5 bolts to 2-bolt anchor.

11. A Fistful of Potash (5.10a) Popular and good. Climb up left past three bolts to a flared finger crack. Pull up to good jams and a 2-bolt anchor on a ledge. 45 feet. **Rack:** Small cams and TCUs.

12. Ralph the Rat (5.11a) Up the steep face right of an arête. 5 bolts to 2-bolt anchor.

13. Mini Me (5.9+) Start left of an overhanging corner. Climb a thin crack past a bolt to a small roof. Continue up a chimney to a 2-bolt anchor. **Rack:** Camalots from #.75 to #3.

The next five routes are left of the *Fistful of Potash* buttress on a clean varnished wall. **Descent:** Rappel or lower from all routes.

Wall Street

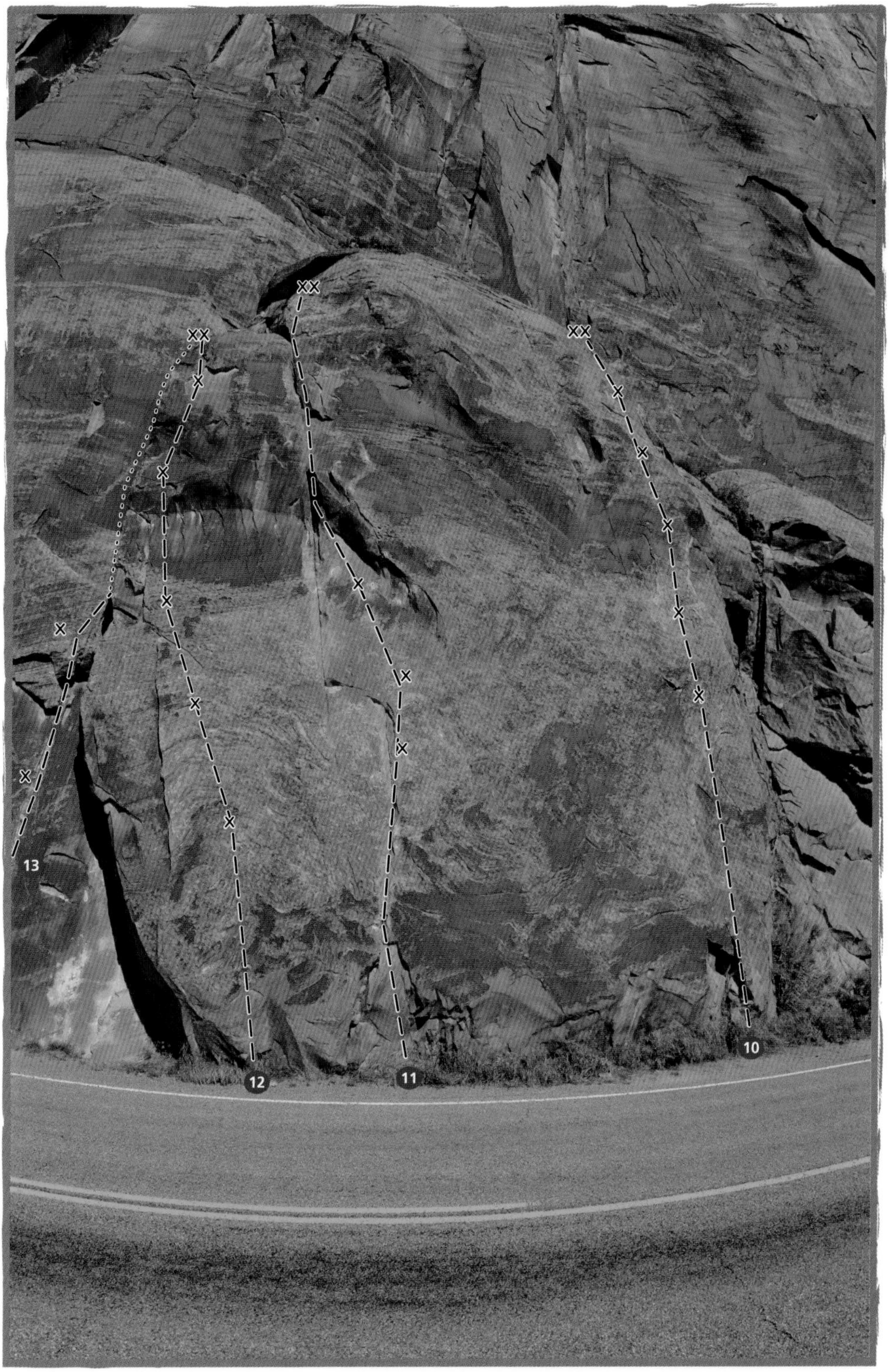

Wall Street

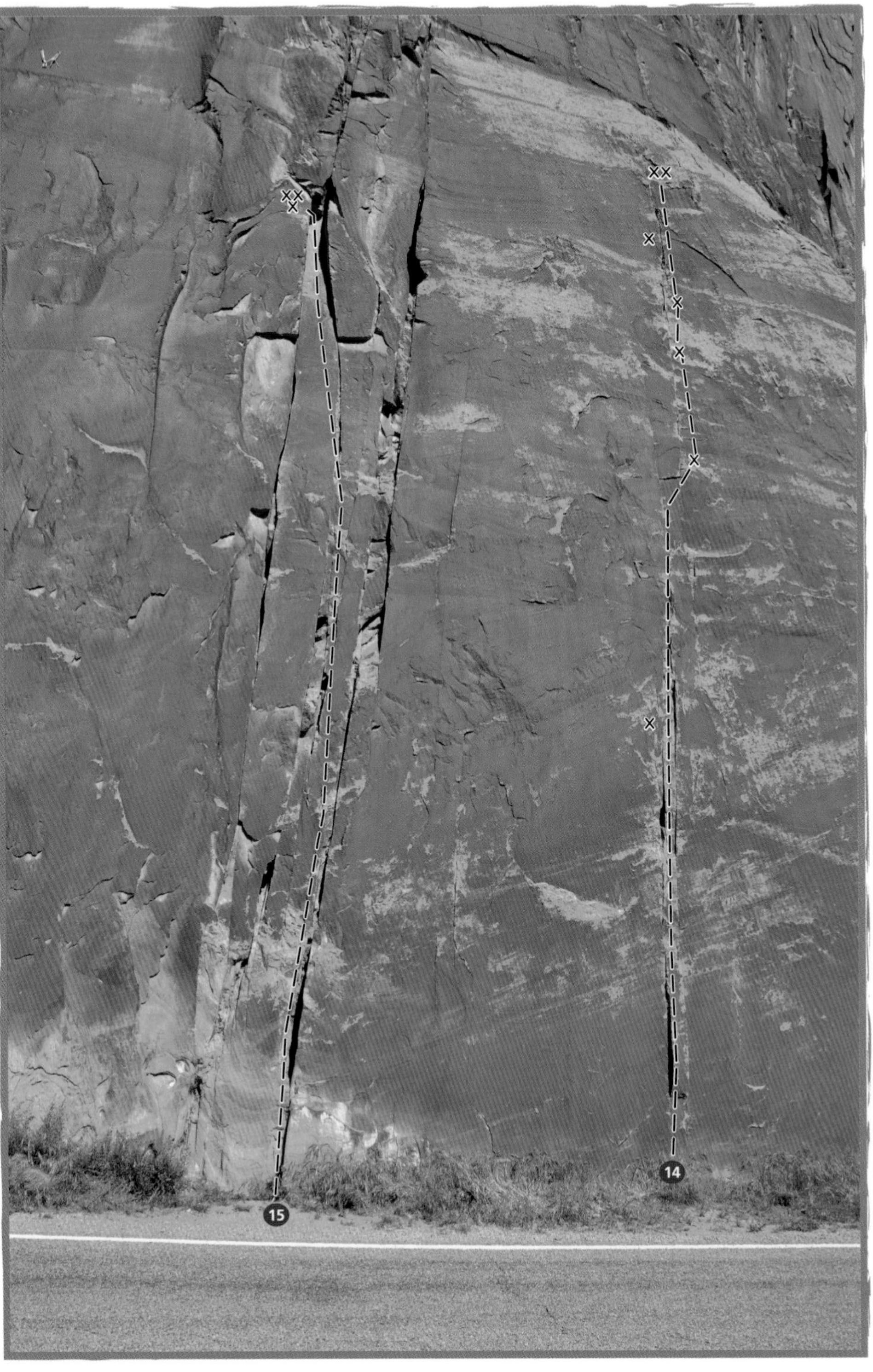

14. Last Tango in Potash (5.11d) Excellent but difficult route up a seam on a steep black slab. Gear protects the hard moves to bolt 1 and the run-out to bolt 2. Find 5.11 cruxes at bolts 1, 2, and 3. 5 bolts to 2-bolt anchor. 60 feet. **Rack:** Small TCUs and Stoppers.

15. Pinhead (5.10b) Fifteen feet left of *Last Tango in Potash.* Climb the left crack in a series of broken crack systems just left of a varnished slab. A set of anchors is at 50 feet and another set at 80 feet. **Rack:** Friends and TCUs.

16. Unknown (5.12b) Climb thin cracks and corners to anchors in black stone. 4 bolts to 2-bolt anchor. **Rack:** TCUs, Stoppers, and small cams.

17. The Potash Sanction (5.11a) Begin in the crack left of *Unknown.* Layback (5.9) up a left-facing corner to a bolt. Work over a roof (5.10c) in the wide crack and continue to a 2-bolt anchor. 70 feet. **Rack:** TCUs, cams to 4 inches, and Stoppers.

18. No Fly Zone (5.12+) Climb *The Potash Sanction* to the roof, then traverse left and work up a thin left-facing corner that becomes a right-facing corner. 7 bolts to 2-bolt anchor. **Rack:** Camalots from #.5 to #3, quickdraws, and a couple slings.

These three routes climb thin right-facing corners next to the road. **Descent:** Rappel or lower from all routes.

Wall Street

19. Astro Lad (5.11a) Excellent, recommended climb up a steep right-facing corner. Jam a thin crack up the corner to a bolt on the outside edge. Hard crack and face climbing leads back into the corner to a 2-bolt anchor. If you stay in the corner all the way, it's 5.11+. **Descent:** Rappel 60 feet. **Rack:** Friends to #2.5 and TCUs.

20. Another Roadside Distraction (5.10b) An obvious right-facing corner 20 feet left of *Astro Lad.* Climb the blocky crack up right to a sustained finger crack to a 3-bolt anchor. Crux is a thin layback. 50 feet. **Rack:** Camalots from #.5 to #2 and TCUs.

21. Chemistry (5.12) Climb *Another Roadside Distraction* to a bolt on the left, then work up left along cracks to an arête and shallow left-facing corner. Climb insecurely to anchors. 4 bolts to 2-bolt anchor. 60 feet. **Rack:** From #00 TCUs to #2 Camalots.

Locate the next two routes on a clean panel with a right-facing dihedral on the left and an arching corner on the right. **Descent:** Rappel or lower from all routes.

Eric Bjørnstad, a longtime climber, developed a passion for Moab and the surrounding red-rock desert in the 1960s. During that time he scaled tottering sandstone spires that most climbers these days would shudder to think about climbing, given the primitive gear, lack of information, and the area's utter remoteness from civilized America. Partnered with pioneer climbers Fred Beckey and Harvey T. Carter, Eric amassed a first-ascent tick list of wild and spooky desert climbs—Echo Tower in the Fisher Towers; The Middle Sister, Eagle Rock Spire, Jacob's Ladder, and Chinle Spire in Monument Valley; Echo Pinnacle and The Bride outside Moab; and Moses and Zeus in Canyonlands National Park.

Wall Street

Wall Street

22. Mother Trucker (5.11) Monkey up a left-facing corner using a variety of layaways, jams, and stems. Crux at the top is a lunge to the anchors. 2-bolt anchor. 60 feet. **Rack:** TCUs to a #2.5 Friend.

23. Napping with the Alien (5.11d/12a) Gymnastic, fingery, and fun. Mantle onto a shelf and climb up right. Crux above bolt 4 is a grade harder for short folks. 5 bolts to 2-bolt anchor. 65 feet.

The next routes, some of the best at Wall Street, are 150 feet left of *Napping with the Alien.* Don't toprope or lower on *Bad Moki Roof* and *Flakes of Wrath;* it damages and grooves the soft stone. **Descent:** Rappel or lower from all routes.

24. Bad Moki Roof (5.9) Fun climb over a large roof. Climb a finger crack in a right-facing dihedral to the roof. Undercling out the roof to an awkward lip encounter. Finish a slabby crack to a 2-bolt anchor. **Descent:** Rappel the route. To avoid rock damage, do not lower or toprope. **Rack:** TCUs, large Stoppers, and Camalots from #.5 to #2.

25. Eyes of Falina (5.9 R) Begin to the left of the large roof. Face climb up left on flakes to a bolt. Continue up left past the left edge of a roof, then

Wall Street

move up right on a slab to a 3-bolt anchor. 90 feet. **Rack:** Medium Stoppers and medium to large cams.

26. Flakes of Wrath (5.9) Popular classic route—one of Wall Street's best climbs. Watch out for poison sumac at the base. Jam and layback a hand crack to thin moves between pockets in the crack (5.9). Undercling left under a roof and finish at a 3-bolt anchor. 75 feet. **Rack:** Double sets of cams from 1 to 3 inches and medium to large Stoppers. (GPS N 38.32.987 / W 109.35.846)

27. Flakes of Wrath Direct (5.11b) A good toprope. Layback and jam thin cracks to a flake face climbing crux.

28. Mississippi Half Step (5.12a) Excellent face route. A crux bouldery start leads to hard face climbing. 5 bolts to 2-bolt anchor.

The next routes are about 250 feet left of the *Flakes of Wrath* sector and right of a deep canyon that slices into the cliff. **Descent:** Rappel or lower from all routes.

29. Frogs of a Feather (5.10c) Begin on tan rock 150 feet right of a parking area. Jam a finger crack flake. At the top, exit up left past a bolt to a left traverse (5.10c). Finish at a 2-bolt anchor on a ledge. 80 feet. **Rack:** TCUs and Friends to #3 with several #1s. (GPS N 38.32.945 / W 109.35.869)

30. Shoot Up or Shut Up (5.11a) Same start as *Frogs of a Feather.* Edge up left and pass three bolts to an arête. Work up the arête (5.11a) to a ledge with a 2-bolt anchor. 5 bolts to 2-bolt anchor. **Rack:** TCUs, small Stoppers, and a #4 Camalot.

31. Shoot Up or Shut Up Corner (5.12a) Tricky climbing up a narrow left-facing corner. Above, work up two broken cracks to anchors. 4 bolts to 2-bolt anchor.

32. Wake of the Flood (5.10c) Climb a thin crack past two bolts to a small roof (5.10c). Finish up a wider crack. 2 bolts to 2-bolt anchor. 60 feet. **Rack:** Sets of Friends, TCUs, and Stoppers.

Wall Street

Wall Street

33. Flash Flood (5.11a) Climb a thin, edgy face protected with three drilled pitons and two bolts to a 2-bolt anchor.

34. Visible Panty Line (5.10a) A good but weird line up four thin cracks. Climb thin cracks past a drilled angle to a belay ledge with a 2-bolt anchor. **Rack:** Small Friends, TCUs, and Stoppers.

35. Pounding the Frog (5.10b) Dicey face climbing to a bolt. Continue up left past another bolt to a 2-bolt anchor. 40 feet.

36. Bolts to Bumpy Land (5.11c) Long, excellent face route right of a deep gully. Grab edges up a tan face, pass a roof on the left, and friction up a black slab to anchors. 15 bolts to 2-bolt anchor. 115 feet. **Descent:** Rappel with two ropes. (GPS N 38.32.935 / W 109.35.885)

The next two routes are in the middle of a long, unbroken cliff band. They ascend a clean alcove of tan rock. **Descent:** Rappel or lower from all routes.

Two common plants found along Wall Street are poison ivy and jimsonweed, or datura. Watch out for poison ivy, which grows in clumps with shiny leaves. Remember: Leaves of three, let it be. Keep your rope, dog, and yourself out of it. Don't be like one climber I saw on a hot day—he was lying in a 3-foot bush to keep cool! Datura has beautiful trumpet-shaped white flowers that open on summer nights and close in the morning. Datura is a potent Native American psychedelic drug, but don't be tempted. People have died ingesting it and animals go crazy, hence its other name—locoweed.

Wall Street

37. Blowing Chunks (5.11b/c) A spectacular line up a thin left-facing corner to the right side of an arch. Stem and edge up the corner and its outside arête (crux between bolts 2 and 3) to an anchor right of the arch. 4 bolts to 2-bolt anchor. 60 feet. **Rack:** Bring many small Stoppers, TCUs or small Aliens, and small cams including a #.75 TCU. (GPS N 38.32.890 / W 109.35.906)

38. Unknown (5.11) A thin bolted face up a clean panel. 7 bolts to 2-bolt anchor.

These three excellent routes are above a pullout. **Descent:** Rappel or lower from all routes.

39. 30 Seconds over Potash (5.8) One of Wall Street's best climbs. Jam and layback a crack in a left-facing dihedral to a 2-bolt anchor. 80 feet. **Rack:** Stoppers, TCUs, and Camalots to #2. (GPS N 38.32.870 / W 109.35.911)

40. Lucy in the Sky with Potash (5.10a) Classic and excellent. Begin 15 feet left of *30 Seconds over Potash.* Stem and jam a crack up the left-facing corner to a 3-bolt anchor. 65 feet. **Rack:** Stoppers, TCUs, and Camalots to #3. (GPS N 38.32.874 / W 109.35.922)

41. Nervous in Suburbia (5.10a) Wall Street's best face route. Tricky face moves up a clean sandstone panel. 4 bolts to 2-bolt anchor. 65 feet. (GPS N 38.32.866 / W 109.35.918)

Wall Street

Sam Higby on *Nervous in Suburbia* at Wall Street. Photo Andrew Burr

42. Under the Boardwalk (5.12a/b) Begin on the right side of a gully 40 feet left of *Nervous in Suburbia.* Hard face climbing leads up an arête and left across a face, then finishes up a blunt prow. 8 bolts to 3-bolt anchor. 60 feet.

The next routes are on a clean panel just left of a deep gully.

43. I Love Loosey (5.11d) Climb a blunt arête and face between tan and black sandstone. 5 bolts to 2-bolt anchor. 50 feet.

44. Fernando (5.11b/c) Excellent and sustained face climb—one of Wall Street's best. Start right of an arête. Pull edges to a final crux at the anchors. 6 bolts to 2-bolt anchor.

45. Baby Blue (5.11a) One of the Street's best cracks. Jam and layback up a beautiful finger crack in a left-facing corner to a 2-bolt anchor. 40 feet. **Rack:** Stoppers, many TCUs, and Friends to #2.5. (GPS N 38.32.845 / W 109.35.926)

Wall Street

45
44
43

46. Snake's Slab (5.8) Popular route on the left side of a gully. Climb to a high first bolt, then friction up the slabby fin. 5 bolts to 2-bolt anchor. 65 feet. (GPS N 38.32.835 / W 109.35.937)

The following routes are just right of the School Room Two sector, a long section of slabs. A large pullout below the cliff offers convenient parking and a five-second approach. **Descent:** Rappel or lower from all routes.

47. Static Cling (5.11a) Great route on the right side of a pullout. Climb a thin crack in a left-facing dihedral to a roof, hand traverse left below the roof, and finish with jams and face holds to a 2-bolt anchor. **Rack:** Stoppers, TCUs, and Friends or Camalots to #3. (GPS N 38.32.812 / W 109.35.950)

48. Potash Bong Hit (5.10) Begin 10 feet left of *Static Cling.* Jam a splitter hand crack up a big detached flake for 30 feet to a wide section. Finish with jams and laybacks to *Static Cling*'s anchors. **Rack:** Camalots from #.5 to #4 with extra #1s and #2s.

Wall Street

49. The Good, the Bad, and the Potash (5.11b) Jam *Potash Bong Hit*'s hand crack, then face climb left and up on good holds. 3 bolts to 2-bolt anchor. **Rack:** Camalots from #.5 to #2 with extra #1s and #2s.

50. Skeletonic (5.11+) Good and popular. Begin at a Russian olive tree. Stem and jam up a thin crack in a right-facing dihedral. 4 bolts to 3-bolt anchor. 70 feet. **Rack:** Medium Stoppers, TCUs, and Friends or Camalots to #2. (GPS N 38.32.807 / W 109.35.954)

The next three routes are on a recessed panel flanked by dihedrals. Park directly beneath the wall.

Wall Street

Wall Street

51. Top Forty (5.8) Jam, stem, and layback up a left-facing corner. 2 bolts to 2-bolt anchor. 45 feet. (GPS N 38.32.804 / W 109.35.959)

52. Unknown (5.11) Thin crack up a face. 6 bolts to 2-bolt anchor. 75 feet. **Rack:** TCUs and small to medium cams.

53. Lacto Mangulation (5.10b) Popular. Climb flakes to a bolt by a thin crack. Grab good edges up left and jam a fist crack in a right-facing dihedral. The crack narrows to fingers; layback and stem to anchors. 3 bolts to 2-bolt anchor. **Rack:** Large cam. (GPS N 38.32.799 / W 109.35.957)

The School Room Two sector, a popular area with topropes and easy leads, begins left of *Lacto Mangulation* and a cottonwood tree. The next routes are on two clean slabs split by a wide crack. **Descent:** Rappel or lower from all routes.

54. Banana Peel (5.10a) Sustained face pitch up the face left of a big tree. Tricky moves lead to a piton 15 feet up. Work up right on a varnished calcite face to anchors. 7 bolts/pitons to 2-bolt anchor.

55. Brown Banana (5.9) Good but the edges are worn. Start just left of *Banana Peel.* Face climb left of a blunt prow. 5 bolts to 3-bolt anchor.

56. Grama and Green Suede Shoes (5.7) Climb a wide low-angle crack. At the top, step left to a 2-bolt anchor. **Rack:** Camalots from #3 to #5. (GPS N 38.32.791 / W 109.35.964)

57. Slab #1 (5.5) Fun route up a slab. 2 bolts to 2-bolt anchor.

Wall Street

58. Slab #2 (5.5) Climb an easy slab. 3 bolts to 3-bolt anchor.

The next few routes are on the left side of the School Room Two sector. **Descent:** Rappel or lower from all routes.

59. Easy Slab (5.4) No topo. Climb a clean low-angle slab flanked on the right by a thin left-facing corner and on the left by a bouldery gully. 2 bolts to 2-bolt anchor.

60. She-La the Peeler (5.9) Good slabbing up a slab on the far left side of the sector. Make tricky moves up right on steep rock, then cruise the upper slab. 7 bolts to 2-bolt anchor. (GPS N 38.32.749 / W 109.35.982)

61. Slab Route (5.7 R) Above the left side of the large pullout and just right of a willow tree. Do a short crux and then smear the nice slab. 9 bolts to 2-bolt anchor. **Descent:** Rappel 90 feet. (GPS N 38.32.745 / W 109.35.986)

The next routes are on the cliff section left of the School Room Two sector. Start the first route just left of a large hackberry tree.

62. Puppy Love (5.9) Good but a bit runout. Angle up right into a grooved seam. Sandy friction smears to anchors. 3 bolts to 2-bolt anchor. 65 feet. **Rack:** TCUs and Friends or Camalots from #.5 to #1.

63. Steel Your Face (5.10a) Brilliant climbing with great pro and dicey sequences. Begin 10 feet left of *Puppy Love.* Friction up a steep white slab. 7 bolts to 3-bolt anchor. 80 feet. (GPS N 38.32.724 / W 109.35.995)

Wall Street

Wall Street

64. Chris-Cross (5.11a R) Climb a left-facing corner (5.9 R) to a bulge, then work out left to a thin face crux with a piton. Go back right into the crack and a crux just below the anchors. 70 feet. **Rack:** Stoppers and Friends to #3.5.

65. Just Another Pretty Face (5.10b R) Interesting and sustained. Face climb (5.8 R) to a bolt 25 feet up. Work up left to a crux at bolt 4. Finish up right to anchors. 6 bolts to 2-bolt anchor. 80 feet. To avoid decking below bolt 1, climb *Chris-Cross* to a #2.5 Friend placement, traverse to bolt 1, then back clean the cam. **Rack:** #2.5 Friend.

66. Don Smurfo (5.10 R) Begin 15 feet left of *Just Another Pretty Face.* Climb a thin crack system to a drilled piton. Face climb up right and join *Pretty Face* at its fourth bolt. **Rack:** Stoppers and TCUs.

67. Big Sky Mud Flaps (5.10d) Excellent, exciting, and sustained. Work up a crack/seam on varnished rock to a bulge and the upper white headwall. 9 bolts/pitons to 2-bolt anchor. **Descent:** Lower 100 feet. Tie a knot in your rope's end. (GPS N 38.32.715 / W 109.35.995)

68. Impasse (5.12+) Start 20 feet left of *Big Sky Mud Flaps.* Face climb up a discontinuous crack/seam on black rock to a bolt. Work up right on steep, thin face climbing and finish up *Big Sky Mud Flaps.* 4 bolts to 2-bolt anchor. **Descent:** Lower 100 feet. **Rack:** TCUs and Friends.

Wall Street

Wall Street

Wall Street

69. Walk on the Wide Side (5.10a) Thrutch up an obvious splitter off-width crack for 80 feet to a 2-bolt anchor just below the horizontal break. One fixed piton protects the crux. 80 feet. **Rack:** Camalots from #.5 to #5. (GPS N 38.32.710 / W 109.35.997)

70. Armageddon (5.12a/b) Desperate face climbing on thin edges and smears. 5 bolts to 2-bolt anchor. 60 feet.

71. Unknown (5.11) Climb along a thin crack to a high first bolt. Continue up the crack and a right-facing corner. 6 bolts to 2-bolt anchor.

72. Jacob's Ladder (5.10d R) Short, thoughtful lead. Edge up a delicate slab to the first bolt. Smear the crux and climb to anchors in varnished rock. 4 bolts to 2-bolt anchor. 50 feet. (GPS N 38.32.703 / W 109.36.001)

73. Shadowfax (5.11a) Left of a bushy crack and right of a steep gully. Dicey slabwork leads to a high first bolt. Edge and friction up right to anchors. Crux is at bolt 4. 5 bolts to 2-bolt anchor. 50 feet. (GPS N 38.32.701 / W 109.36.005)

74. Potstash (5.9) Fun and well protected. Start left of the gully. Grab good edges up fractured rock to a high crux. 5 bolts to 2-bolt anchor.

Wall Street

Maverick Buttress

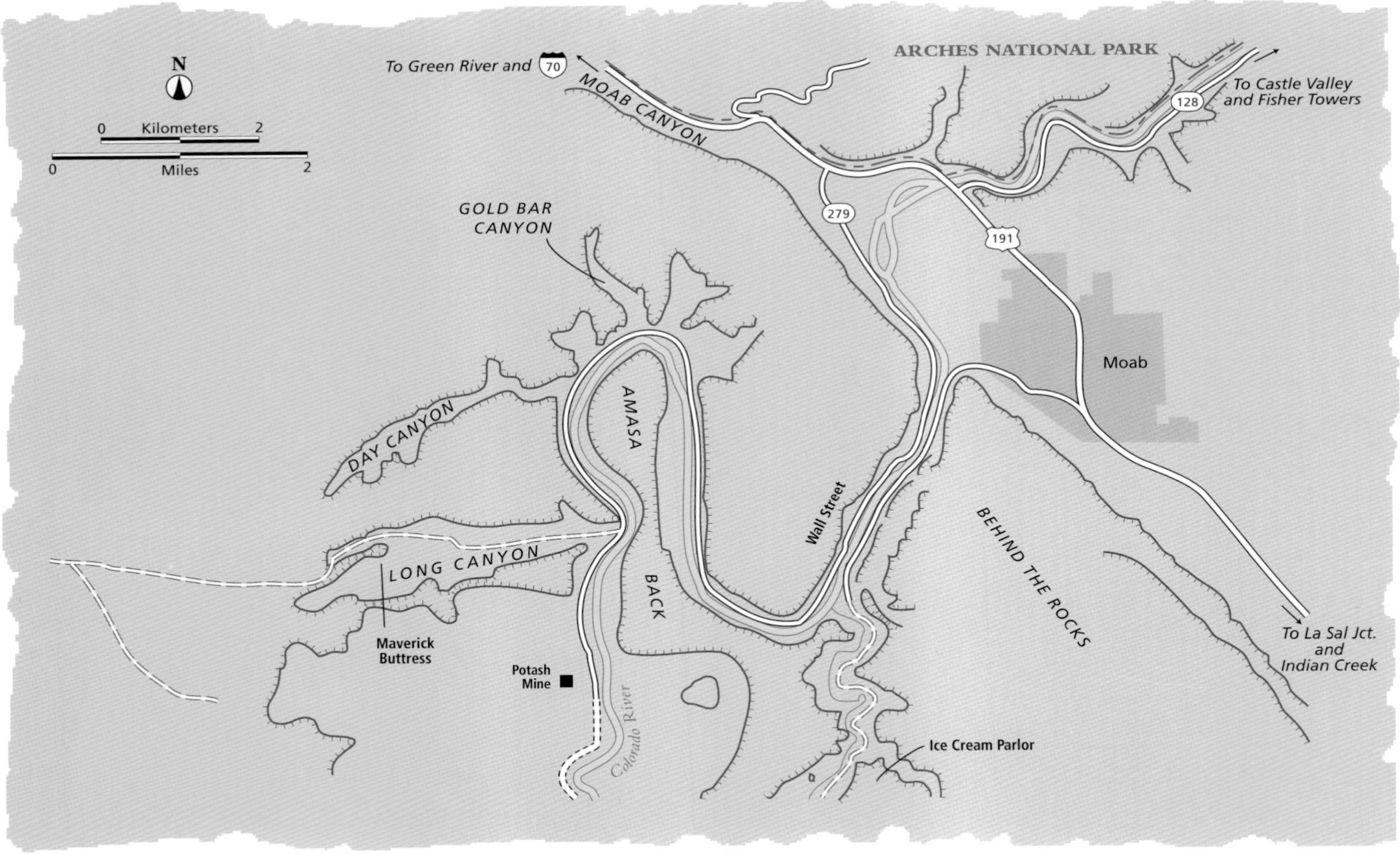
N
0 Kilometers 2
0 Miles 2
To Green River and 70
MOAB CANYON
ARCHES NATIONAL PARK
To Castle Valley and Fisher Towers
128
279
191
Moab
GOLD BAR CANYON
DAY CANYON
AMASA
BACK
Wall Street
BEHIND THE ROCKS
LONG CANYON
Maverick Buttress
Potash Mine
Colorado River
Ice Cream Parlor
To La Sal Jct. and Indian Creek

4.

Maverick Buttress

Maverick Buttress, an east- and south-facing Wingate sandstone cliff, perches near the head of 4-mile-long Long Canyon, a broad cliff-lined canyon that drops east from the Island in the Sky to the Colorado River. The cliff offers not only the finest assortment of crack climbs near Moab but also the best scenic vista of any area crag, with distant views of Behind the Rocks and the La Sal Mountains. Most of the climbs were established by Jack Roberts and Charlie Fowler in 1987.

Maverick is reached by Long Canyon Road, a narrow dirt road that climbs from Potash Road and the Colorado River to the cliff just below the mesa top. The road is passable for two-wheel-drive vehicles except in wet and snowy weather. It's best to use a high-clearance vehicle if possible. Don't camp at the parking area or disturb the water tank above the road. It's a critical watering tank for desert bighorn sheep.

Getting there: Long Canyon is 15 miles south of US 191, west of Moab. Drive north from Moab on US 191 for a couple miles to the Potash Road turnoff (GPS N 38.32.796 / W 109.38.880). Turn left (south) here onto paved Potash Road (UT 279) and drive 15 miles to Long Canyon. Turn right (west) off the highway onto dirt Long Canyon Road. Drive 3.4 miles up the narrow road to a parking area at the top of the switchbacks (GPS N 38.32.780 / W 109.41.796). A short trail climbs west to the buttress from the parking area. Hiking time from car to cliff is five minutes. The first three routes face the road. Routes are described from right to left.

Charlie Fowler and Jack Roberts did the first ascents of all the best routes at Maverick Buttress in January 1987. "Charlie drove all around the Moab desert the year before," Jack says, "and found the cliff. We were really into watching *Gunsmoke* reruns then so we named all the routes with a *Gunsmoke* theme. We both liked Miss Kitty too so we named some after her."

1. Rawhide (5.11d) Jam a crack past a wide section with a flake. Continue up the wide crack past a couple pods. Finish with a finger and thin hand crack to a 2-bolt anchor on a small ledge. **Descent:** Rappel or lower 115 feet. **Rack:** Four sets of Friends or Camalots.

2. Miss Kitty Likes It That Way (5.11d) Excellent thin crack climb. Jam a hand crack that narrows to fingers to a flared rest niche. Tricky jams exit the pod. Finish with wide fingers (5.11d) to a 3-bolt anchor. **Rack:** Double Friends through #2.5 and a set of TCUs. **Descent:** Rappel or lower 70 feet.

3. Gunsmoke (5.11a) One of Moab's best climbs up a perfect splitter! Start atop a boulder. Jam a hand crack up the right side of a flake (left start is 5.11c). Continue up the hand crack to a pod rest. Finish up cruxy finger-locks in the final thin crack. **Descent:** Make a 115-foot rappel or lower from a 3-bolt anchor. Use a 70-meter rope to jam and lower. **Rack:** Friends or equivalent including two #.75s, one #1, two #1.5s, two #2s, five #2.5s (use a couple #3s if you don't have enough #2.5s), one #3, one #3.5, and possibly a #4.

The following routes are on the south wall of Maverick Buttress. Access them by hiking up a trail that heads up left from the parking area to the cliff base or by squeezing through a hole left of *Gunsmoke.*

CJ Sidebottom jamming up *Tequila Sunrise* at Maverick Buttress.

Maverick Buttress

Maverick Buttress

4. Boothill (5.12b) Begin left of a juniper tree. Jam a thin hands to fat-finger crack (2 inches) up a leaning right-facing dihedral into a pod with loose blocks. Grovel to a drilled piton below a roof. Jam a sustained, steep fat-finger crack and thin hand crack (5.12) to a 2-bolt anchor. **Descent:** Rappel 100 feet. **Rack:** Two or three sets of Friends or Camalots with extra #2 and #1.5 Friends.

5. Clantons in the Dust (5.10d) A wide and wild Jimmie Dunn special. Start below a right-facing dihedral. Work up a wide chimney filled with blocks. Jam a crack to a strenuous off-width section. Finish up a reasonable crack to a 2-bolt anchor on the left wall. **Descent:** Rappel 100 feet with two ropes. **Rack:** Lots of wide stuff—Big Bros, #4 and #5 Camalots, and Camalots from #.75 to #3.

6. High Noon (5.11a/b) Short, sustained, and thuggish. Jam a fingertip crack (5.11a/b) for 35 feet to a 2-bolt anchor. Layback the route (5.10d) if toproping. **Rack:** Stoppers and TCUs. **Descent:** Lower 35 feet.

7. Tequila Sunrise (5.10d) Another of Moab's best crack climbs. Start atop a boulder. Jam the obvious splitter crack on the right wall of a right-facing dihedral. Jam the thin hands crux, which widens to perfect hands to a rest pod. Look for occasional footholds on the face. Above the pod, angle up left on wide hands to the top of the dihedral. Finish with an off-width to a 3-bolt anchor with chains. **Descent:** Rappel or lower 80 feet. **Rack:** Two or three sets of Friends from #1.5 to #4, with extra #2.5s to #3.5s. A #4 Camalot is useful at the top.

8. Hot Toddy (5.10a/b) Superb, sustained hand jamming with stemming rests. Start on the left side of a boulder. Awkward moves lead into the black right-facing dihedral. Jam perfect hands up the vertical dihedral to a final off-width section and a 3-bolt anchor with chains. **Descent:** Rappel or lower 80 feet. **Rack:** Friends including four #3s, four #3.5s, and three #4s or lots of #2, #3, and #3.5 Camalots; also two #4 Camalots for the bottom and top.

Find the next three routes by following a trail west from *Hot Toddy* along the cliff base to a cul-de-sac. The first two routes are on the right and the third is on the left.

9. Texas Two Step (5.10a/b) Excellent and one of the cliff's easier cracks. Locate a beautiful crack up a right-facing then left-facing corner. Jam a hand to fist crack up the white right-facing corner, then continue up the left-facing corner to a 2-bolt anchor. **Descent:** Rappel 70 feet. **Rack:** Double sets of Friends from #2 to #4 with extra #3s, #3.5s, and #4s or double set of Camalots from #.75 to #3.5 plus a #4.

10. Round Up (5.11a) Scramble through boulders left of *Texas Two Step* to the base of a thin crack. Jam parallel finger cracks (5.11a) to a hand crack. Jam to a break, reach right, and finish up a wide hand crack to a 2-bolt anchor. **Descent:** Rappel or lower 80 feet. **Rack:** TCUs (Green Aliens) for the start; Camalots #.5 and #.75 and doubles from #1 to #3.

11. Saddle Sores (5.10) No topo. On the wall opposite *Round Up*. Jam a hand crack in a left-facing corner to a huecoed wall and a final squeeze chimney. End at a 2-piton anchor. **Descent:** Rappel 50 feet. **Rack:** Double Friends from #3 to #4 or double Camalots #2 and #3 plus some wide gear for the top.

Climb gently and consciously on the soft sandstone cliffs surrounding Moab. The sandstone layers—Cutler, Wingate, Entrada, and Navajo—we climb upon are fragile and easily impacted. Many routes have been irreparably damaged by the repeated placement and removal of pitons. Popular crack climbs have worn edges and grooves from repeated foot jams. Don't place additional bolts, and use slings on rappel anchors that match the color of the rock. Also use colored chalk instead of white, which creates visible stains. The national parks require colored chalk. Climb lightly and reduce your impact—it's the right thing to do.

Maverick Buttress

Ice Cream Parlor

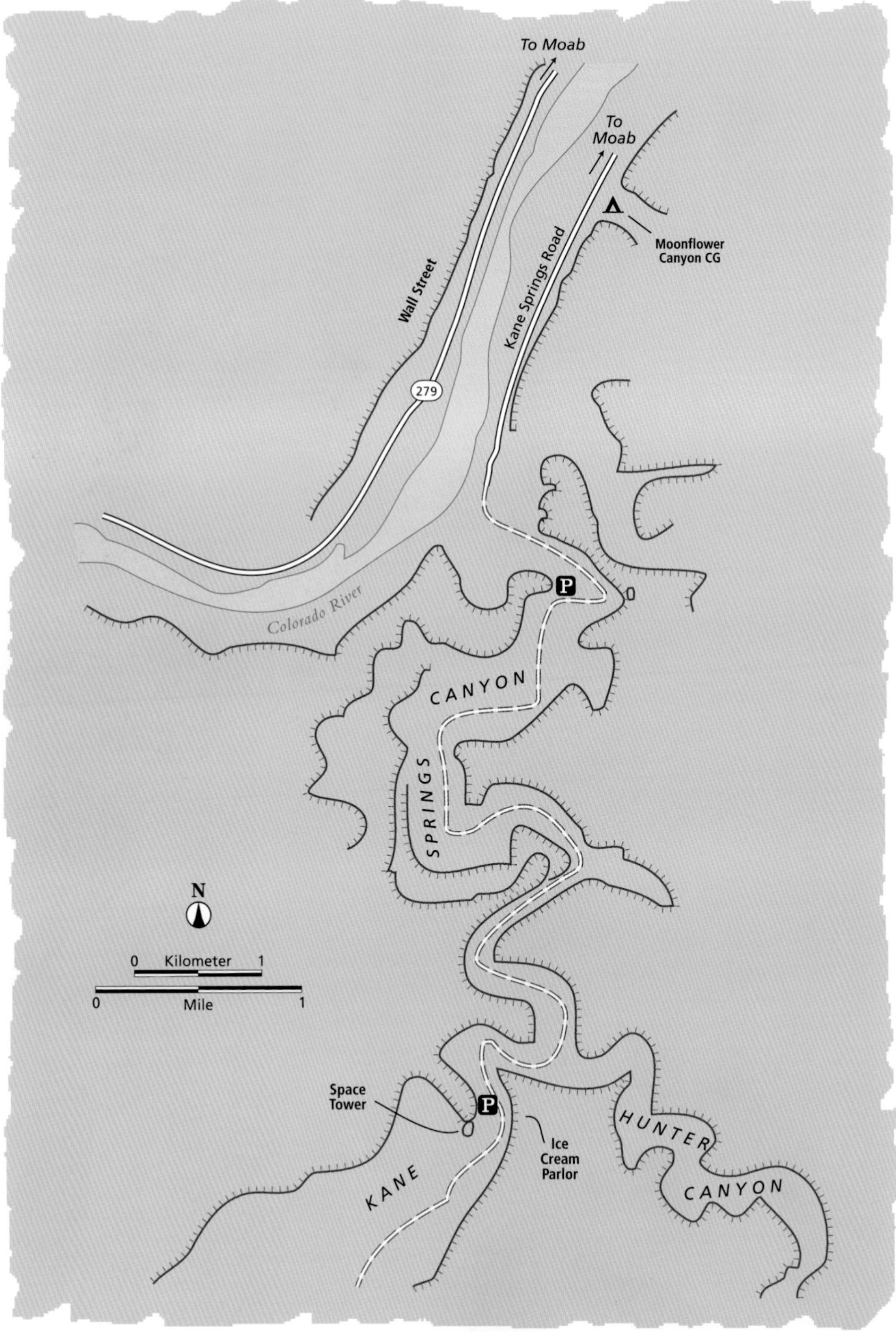
To Moab
To Moab
Moonflower Canyon CG
Wall Street
Kane Springs Road
279
Colorado River
CANYON
SPRINGS
N
0 Kilometer 1
0 Mile 1
Space Tower
Ice Cream Parlor
HUNTER
CANYON
KANE

5.

Ice Cream Parlor

The Ice Cream Parlor is a fine southwest-facing cliff that towers above the east side of the road just before the canyon opens into broad Kane Valley. All of the routes except *Wolverine* ascend a lower tier of varnished Wingate sandstone below the steep, fractured upper face. The right side offers some great crack climbs while the popular left slab has lots of good bolted sport routes and three fun cracks. The one-pitch climbs have bolt anchors for convenient lowers. The cliff is ideal during warmer months since it stays shady in the morning, while in cooler months it soaks up lots of sun. It's usually too hot in summer for comfort. The Ice Cream Parlor is popular, especially on weekends. Come early or climb late.

Getting there: From Main Street (US 191) on the south side of Moab, turn west onto Kane Creek Boulevard at the McDonald's restaurant and drive west to a Y junction. Keep left on the paved road, which becomes Kane Springs Road. Follow it south along the Colorado River to a cattle guard at the canyon entrance. Continue south on the narrow dirt road for 3.6 miles from the cattle guard and park along the right shoulder or in a pullout on the left below the cliff (GPS N 38.50.857 / W 109.59.951). From the right side of a boulder jumble, follow a rough path to the lowest part of the cliff, then hike up left to the slab routes. Hiking time is five minutes. Routes are listed from right to left.

Bill Springer works up *Crack 1* at the Ice Cream Parlor.

Ice Cream Parlor

1. Knee Grinder (5.9+) Begin on the right side. Work up a wide crack system in a right-facing dihedral to a squeeze section to a ledge. Finish up an awkward chimney with a bolt to a 2-bolt anchor. **Descent:** Rappel 75 feet from anchors. **Rack:** Medium to large cams and a Big Bro for the top.

2. The Possessed (5.11c/d) Fun face route up a blunt arête. Funky moves lead left onto the arête. Follow bolts and good edges to anchors on a ledge. Make sure your carabiner doesn't hit the edge below bolt 2. 6 bolts to 2-bolt anchor (same as *Knee Grinder*). 75 feet.

3. The Coffin (5.9) Burly crack climb. Begin on a wide, rocky ledge. Fist jam up broken cracks over a roof. Work up a widening crack to a squeeze chimney in a right-facing dihedral to a 2-bolt anchor. **Descent:** Rappel 75 feet. **Rack:** Small nuts, TCUs, and Camalots to #6 (or Big Bros).

4. Pulp Friction (5.11) Excellent and sustained. Begin on the ledge left of a left-facing corner. Thin face moves lead up right to a bolt. Work right into the steep corner. Climb a few feet before exiting right onto an arête. Face climb past two bolts to anchors. 5 bolts to 2-bolt anchor. **Descent:** Rappel 70 feet. **Rack:** Medium to large cams.

5. Ice Cream Parlor Crack (5.11a) Classic crack—one of the cliff's best climbs. Toprope it by climbing *Good Day to Die.* Start left of *Pulp Friction* on the ledge. Face climb into a right-facing corner. Jam, layback, and stem to a 2-bolt anchor. **Descent:** Rappel 70 feet. **Rack:** TCUs—one #.3, four to five #.4s, two to three #.5s, small cams, and a #4 or #5 Camalot.

6. Good Day to Die (5.9) Fun route up a right-angling dihedral 25 feet left of *Ice Cream Parlor Crack.* Jam and layback the dihedral to a couple bolts on a high slab. **Descent:** Rappel 70 feet. Set up a toprope on the *Parlor Crack* from here. **Rack:** Set of cams to 3 inches.

7. Pork Soda (5.9) Climb *Good Day to Die* to the first bolt, then launch up left over a roof. Finish up a flake crack to a 2-bolt anchor. **Rack:** Set of cams. **Descent:** Rappel from bolt anchors.

The following routes are on a dark varnished slab left of the crack sector. Follow a path along the cliff base to the routes. **Descent:** Rappel or lower from bolt anchors.

"As for me, I'll take Moab, Utah. I don't mean the town itself, of course, but the country which surrounds it—the canyonlands. The slickrock desert. The red dust and burnt cliffs and the lonely sky—all that which lies beyond the end of the roads." —Edward Abbey

Ice Cream Parlor

8. Freezer Burn (5.10a/b) Right side of the slab. Scramble to a ledge, then climb a short right-facing corner to a 2-bolt slab. Follow a broken crack and corner up right to a pod and a final smearing slab split by a thin crack. 90 feet.

9. Night Light (5.10a) Recommended. Climb easy rock to a break (#3 Camalot). Edge and smear up a black slab to anchors above a left-facing corner. 7 bolts to 2-bolt anchor.

10. Vanilla Cream (5.10+) Climb a broken crack to a right-slanting crack. Finish up the left-facing corner with foot smears. 2 bolts to 2-bolt anchor. **Rack:** Stoppers and small to medium cams.

11. RP City (5.10) Hairline crack on the smooth slab. Start up *Vanilla Cream,* but then edge and smear directly up a thin crack to anchors to the left at the break. **Rack:** Fistful of RPs and small Stoppers.

What is a tower? Every serious desert climber offers a different definition. For some it's a freestanding pinnacle. For others it can be semi-detached or have its own summit. I like the definition that my friends Ralph Ferrara and Eve Tallman, longtime Moab climbers, use: "A tower has 5th-class climbing, is freestanding, and you know it when you see it." For the record, as of 2010, Ralph has climbed 270 towers, and Eve over 200!

Ice Cream Parlor

12. Hot Karl Sunday (5.10c) Fun balancy route. Climb a black slab to a long thin roof. Edge past the roof and smear up left, then finish up a cool right-facing corner. 9 bolts to 2-bolt anchor.

13. Crack 1 (5.8) Excellent. Right-hand crack in the slab's center. Good climbing up the crack to anchors at the break atop the slab. **Descent:** Rappel 75 feet. **Rack:** Stoppers, TCUs, and small cams.

14. Wolverine (5.11) Wild climb up the wall above the slab. **Pitch 1:** Climb *Crack 1* and belay at the anchor. **Pitch 2:** Work up a corner on a steep, streaked wall (two bolts) and jam over a big roof to a 2-bolt anchor. **Pitch 3:** Work up the corner above, pass another roof, and end at a 2-bolt belay/rappel station. **Descent:** Rappel the route. **Rack:** Stoppers, TCUs, and cams to 3 inches.

15. Crack 2 (5.8+ R) Fun climbing up the middle crack. Climb directly up the slab or climb broken blocks up *Crack 1* and traverse left to the crack. Finish up the crack to anchors to the right or left. **Rack:** Stoppers, TCUs, and small cams.

16. Crack 3 (5.8) More great climbing. Face climb up right past bolts, then cruise the fun crack. 3 bolts to 2-bolt anchor. **Rack:** Stoppers, TCUs, and small cams.

17. Black and Tan Slab (5.7+) Fun face climbing up the black and tan slab. 4 bolts to 2-bolt anchor.

18. Black Slab (5.7) Climb directly up varnished rock to a shelf. Continue up good rock to anchors. 6 bolts to 2-bolt anchor. For an easier start, begin to the left and climb up right (5.6) past a couple bolts.

19. Brewed Awakenings (5.5) Climb the easy groove to a 2-bolt anchor. **Rack:** Medium cams.

20. Left Slab (5.7) Fun easy route up the slab left of a groove. 4 bolts to 2-bolt anchor.

21. Parlor Game (5.9) On the left side of the far slab. A tricky start to good edges. Finish with committing moves above the last bolt. 3 bolts to 2-bolt anchor.

22. Top-Rope (5.9+) Stout little toprope climb on the left side. Climb the adjoining routes to set up your anchor.

23. Corner Crack (5.6) Great intro to jamming. On the far left side of the sector. Climb a nice hand crack just right of a right-facing dihedral to a 2-bolt anchor. A second pitch climbs up right then back left up short headwalls to a 2-bolt anchor on a ledge. **Rack:** Medium cams.

Space Tower

This semi-detached tower stands a few feet away from the main cliff across the canyon from the Ice Cream Parlor. From a distance the summit appears to rest against the main cliff but is separated by a gap. An excellent route climbs the chimney facing the Parlor. This is not a good climb for moderate leaders because the chimney is runout in spots and has injury potential from a fall. It can be done in one pitch with careful use of runners for rope drag.

Approach: Access the tower by parking along the road below the Ice Cream Parlor (GPS N 38.50.857 / W 109.59.951). Cross Kane Creek and scramble up talus slopes to the base of the chimney on the tower's east side.

24. Hallow Souls (5.9) 2 pitches. No topo. Climb easy rock to the chimney and a crack system on the main wall inside the chimney. Belay here or on a ledge partway up the chimney. Stem up the wide chimney to a bolt. Eventually step left onto the tower and finish up an exposed hand crack to a 2-bolt anchor. Climb onto the summit to tag up, then downclimb back to the anchors. **Descent:** Rappel 165 feet down the route with two ropes. **Rack:** Sets of TCUs and Camalots along with extra slings and two ropes.

Lighthouse Tower

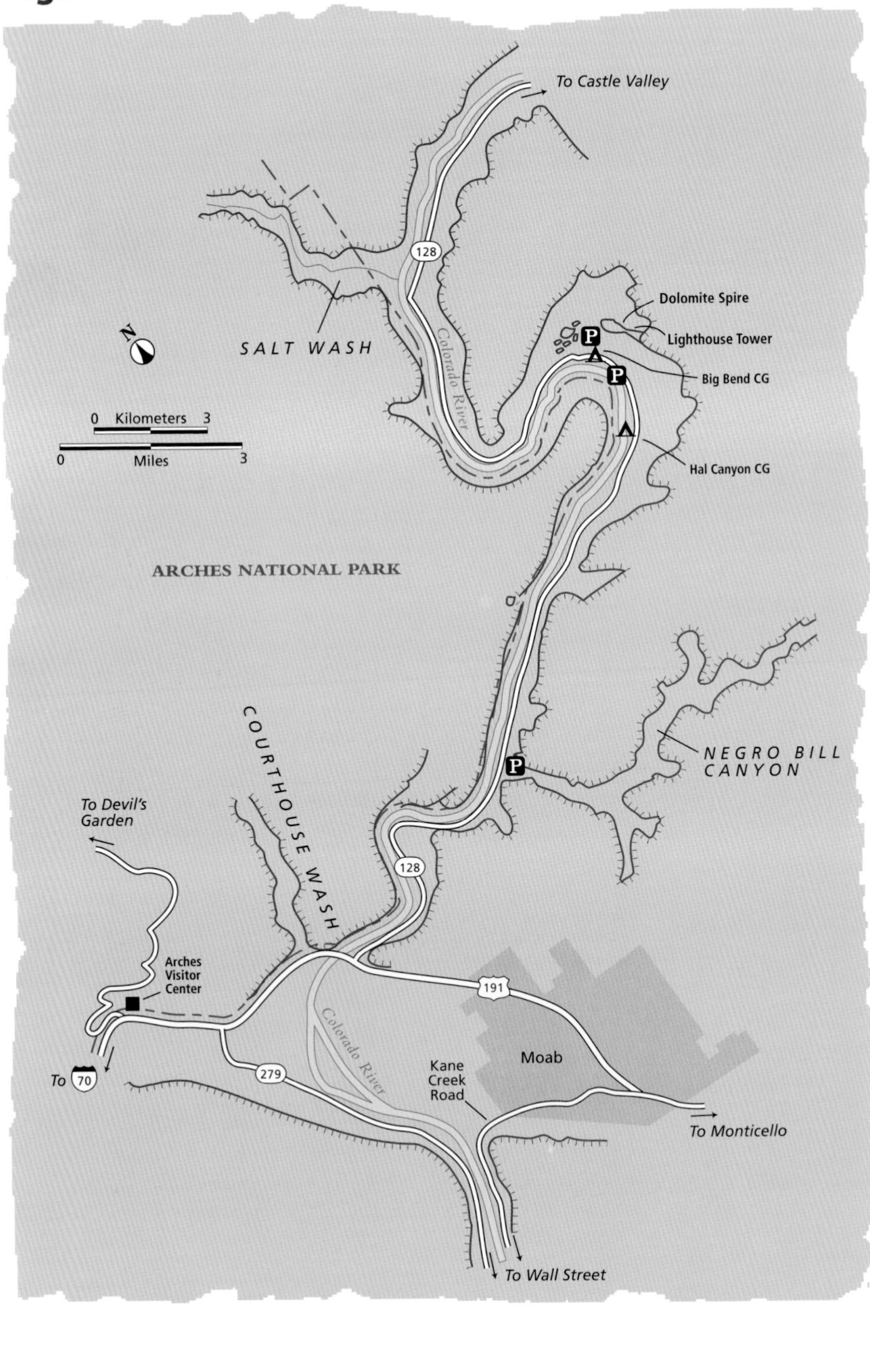

6.

Lighthouse Tower

Lighthouse Tower is a 315-foot-high tower perched on a ridge above River Road, northeast of Moab. The Light-house, one of the best tower climbs near Moab, is a bizarrely shaped, blocky tower topped by a weird ball summit that requires unprotected climbing or trickery to stand on its top. The tiny summit holds only one person at a time. Next to the Light-house are slender Dolomite Spire and Big Bend Butte. The described route, *Lonely Vigil,* is one of the best climbs on the tower. It ascends the side opposite the highway.

Getting there: From Moab, drive north on US 191 and turn right (east) onto UT 128, River Road. Drive east on River Road for 7.5 miles to Big Bend, a huge Colorado River bend. The Lighthouse and Dolomite tow-ers are obvious to the east above the road. Lighthouse is the smaller one on the right; Dolomite Spire is on the left. Continue up the highway past the towers and park on the west side of the road in a pullout just north of a large roadside boulder (GPS N 38.38.797 / W 109.28.601).

There are two ways to reach Lighthouse Tower from here. The best way is to walk down the highway a couple hundred feet and locate a climber's trail, which begins on the east side of the highway (GPS N 38.38.776 / W 109.28.582). The start is marked with a cairn. Hike up talus slopes on the trail, marked with cairns, to the base of the Lighthouse. Approach time is twenty-five to forty minutes. Stay on the existing trail to avoid damaging soils and creating erosion. Alternatively, hike up the can-yon behind the Lighthouse and climb talus slopes to the tower base.

1. Lonely Vigil (II 5.10- R) One of Moab's best tower climbs. This excel-lent route ascends the back (east) side of Lighthouse Tower opposite the road. Follow the access trail to the base of the river side of the Lighthouse. Do a short pitch (5.7) up blocky rock to the notch on the right (south) side of the tower. Belay from a 2-bolt anchor. Follow ledges around the east side of the tower to the base of a deep slot/chimney system on the right side. **Pitch 1:** Jam a hand crack up a corner and over a bulge (5.10-). Continue up a hand crack in a corner to a ledge belay on the left wall of a wide chimney. 140 feet. **Pitch 2:** Continue up a thin hand crack on the

Lighthouse Tower

left side of the chimney to a rappel anchor. Work up the strenuous overhanging stem box above (5.10-), using small nuts and TCUs for pro. At the top, escape left to a shelf and climb to a narrow, exposed belay ledge with a 3-bolt anchor. 130 feet. **Pitch 3:** Make a traverse left and climb (5.9) past a bolt to a 2-bolt anchor below the summit. 40 feet. **Pitch 4:** Unprotected face climbing leads to a summit mantle (5.8 R). Stand on the airy ball, then downclimb back to the belay. No anchors are on the summit. It is possible to haul a rope over the top to set up a toprope. Some protection is found below the summit block. **Descent:** Three rappels down the route. **Rappel 1:** 50 feet from the upper anchors to the notch anchors. **Rappel 2:** 100 feet to anchors in the middle of pitch 2. **Rappel 3:** 165 feet to the ground. Walk back south to the notch on the south side and make a 50-foot rappel to the base of the river side. Be careful pulling your ropes on rappel 2—they can get stuck. An alternative rappel route goes down left from the top of pitch 3. Make two double-rope rappels to the notch. **Rack:** Two sets of Camalots or Friends to #3, a #4 Camalot, sets of Stoppers and TCUs, and RPs for pitch 2.

Chris Hill on the second pitch of *Lonely Vigil* on Lighthouse Tower.
PHOTO ERIC ODENTHAL

Castle Valley Towers

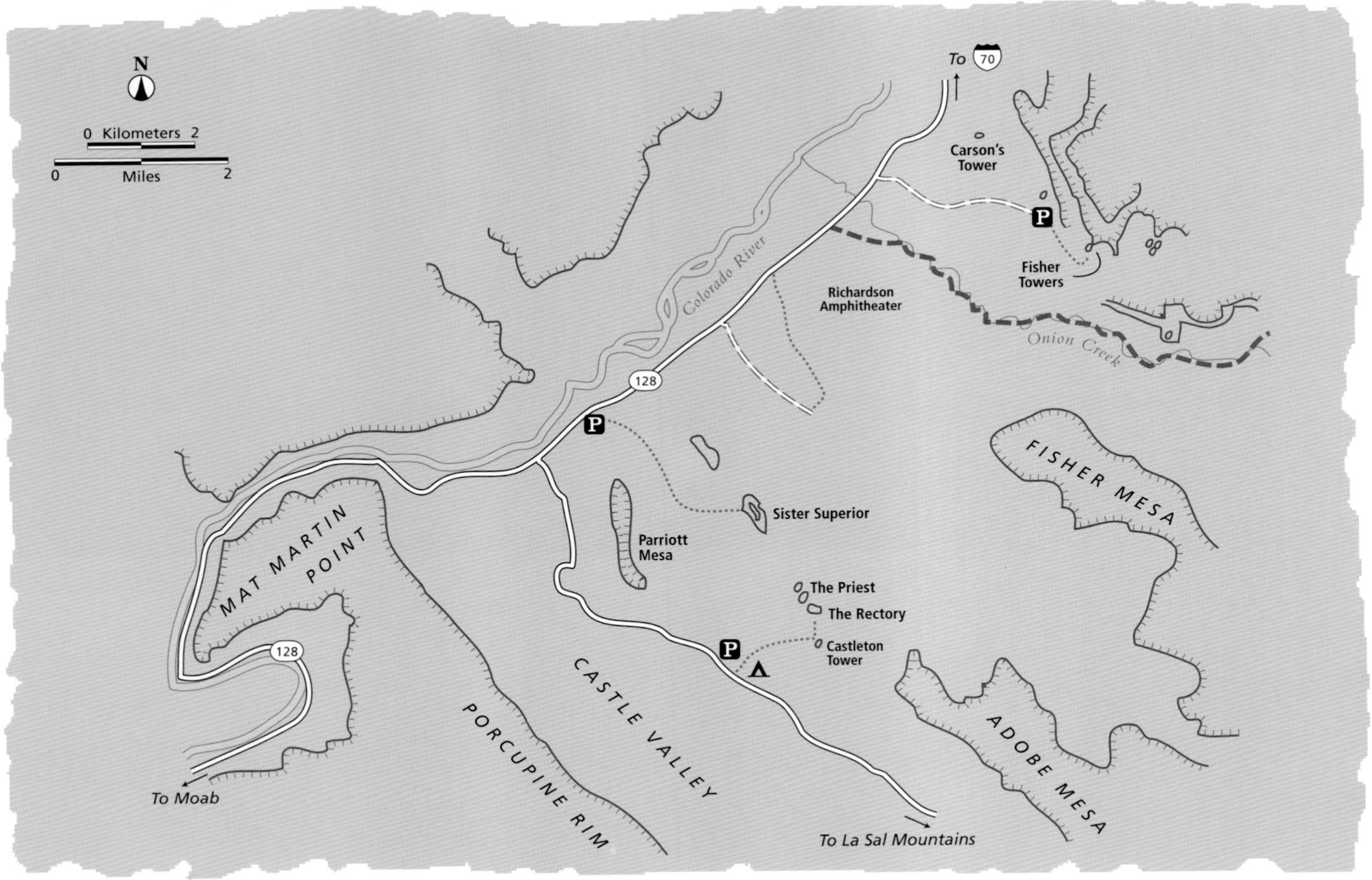
N
0 Kilometers 2
0 Miles 2
To 70
Carson's Tower
P
Fisher Towers
Colorado River
Richardson Amphitheater
Onion Creek
128
P
Sister Superior
Parriott Mesa
FISHER MESA
MAT MARTIN POINT
128
The Priest
The Rectory
Castleton Tower
P
To Moab
PORCUPINE RIM
CASTLE VALLEY
ADOBE MESA
To La Sal Mountains

7.

Castle Valley Towers

The Colorado River, entrenched in a deep sandstone canyon, and broad Castle Valley draining north from the La Sal Mountains, lie east of Moab. A ragged line of towering buttes and towers borders the eastern edge of Castle Valley, forming the canyon country's most spectacular collection of towers.

These buttes and towers, including Castleton Tower, The Rectory, The Priest, and Sister Superior, are Moab's best adventure climbing area. Castleton, at the south end of Castle Ridge, is the most popular big desert tower. Classic routes ascend each of its four faces, ending on a square summit with breathtaking views of the surrounding canyon country. A couple routes—*North Chimney* and *Kor-Ingalls*—are the easiest climbs to the summit of a major tower. These routes are often busy. Come early in the morning or climb during the week to avoid other climbers.

The Rectory, the narrow butte north of Castleton, offers a spectacular free climb—*Fine Jade*—up its exposed south prow. The 330-foot Priest, standing apart north of The Rectory, is climbed by a wild route with a bit of everything, including a huge chimney and airy free climbing to its small summit.

Farther north on Castle Ridge are the Sister Superior spires, a collection of blocky spires locally called The Professor and The Students, and the Convent, a narrow butte. Sister Superior, the tallest tower, offers an excellent route up its sunny southwest face.

You can climb year-round on the Castle Ridge towers. Spring and fall are the best seasons for climbing. Watch out for strong winds, especially in spring, on the high exposed towers. Summers are hot, especially on the south-facing routes. Carry lots of water and keep an eye out for severe thunderstorms, which build up on summer afternoons in July and August. Lightning is a serious danger.

The name Castleton Tower was given by geologist and climber Huntley Ingalls, who first saw the tower in 1956. He was unaware that its local name, still used by Moabites, and the name given on USGS maps is Castle Rock.

One climber was killed on the summit of Castleton by a lightning strike. Winter days can be cold, snowy, and windy, but sunny days often occur.

Descent off all the towers is by rappelling. Numerous rappel stations with excellent modern bolts are found on all the routes. Double-check any webbing and replace if necessary. Tie knots in the ends of your ropes because some of the rappels are long. Be careful not to dislodge rocks when rappelling or pulling your ropes since climbers are often below you. Although some tower descents can be accomplished with a 60-meter (200-foot) or 70-meter rope, plan on bringing two ropes unless you're sure of the rappels.

Getting there: From Moab, drive north on US 191 and turn right (east) onto UT 128, River Road. Drive east on UT 128 for just over 15 miles. Turn right (south) onto Castle Valley Road between mile markers 15 and 16. Follow the paved road for 4.7 miles and turn left into a parking area for the Castleton Tower Primitive Climber's Camp and the trailhead for the Castleton Tower Trail.

Follow the trail up a shallow slot canyon to the top of a hill. Drop down left along an old road and reach an obvious trail. Hike the trail up steep talus slopes to a trail junction north of Castleton Tower. The trail is about 1.5 miles long and takes an hour of hiking to reach this junction.

Go right on a narrow path to reach the base of Castleton's south face. Go left along a ridge to the base of *Fine Jade* on The Rectory. Continue hiking north along the base of The Rectory to reach the base of The Priest's west face.

Castleton Tower

Castleton Tower, a blocky 400-foot-high tower, is the most famous of Utah's sandstone pinnacles. Castleton, also called Castle Rock, sits atop a 1,000-foot-high cone of banded cliffs broken by steep scree and

> Huntley Ingalls and Layton Kor made the first ascent of Castleton on September 14 and 15, 1961. Huntley later wrote in a letter to longtime desert climber Eric Bjørnstad that he was "the first climber to note Castleton Tower, Fisher Towers, and North Six Shooter Peak. This was in 1956 while on a gravity survey of the Colorado Plateau with the Geological Survey. I dreamed of climbing them, but they were beyond reach at that time. After I moved to Boulder in 1959 I tried to interest climbers in these towers, but amazingly I could get no serious response for two years. Finally one day Layton simply said, 'Let's go look at that tower you keep talking about.'"

boulder-strewn slopes. The tower, composed of Wingate sandstone, offers many climbing routes. Included here are the three best routes, including the *Kor-Ingalls Route,* first climbed by famed climbers Layton Kor and Huntley Ingalls in 1961.

Castleton's climbs follow crack systems, offering lots of varied jamming. Grades are hand-size dependent, especially on the *North Face.* The routes can be very busy, especially on spring and autumn weekends. Use extreme caution if other parties are ahead of you or rappelling. Like any sandstone cliff, loose rock abounds. Wear a helmet to protect your head.

Descent: Descent is by rappel. The *Kor-Ingalls Route* can have a lot of traffic, so don't rappel it if others are climbing since you'll be sharing the same anchors. It's best to make three rappels from bolt anchors down the *North Face* to avoid congestion. As always, don't dislodge rocks onto anyone below.

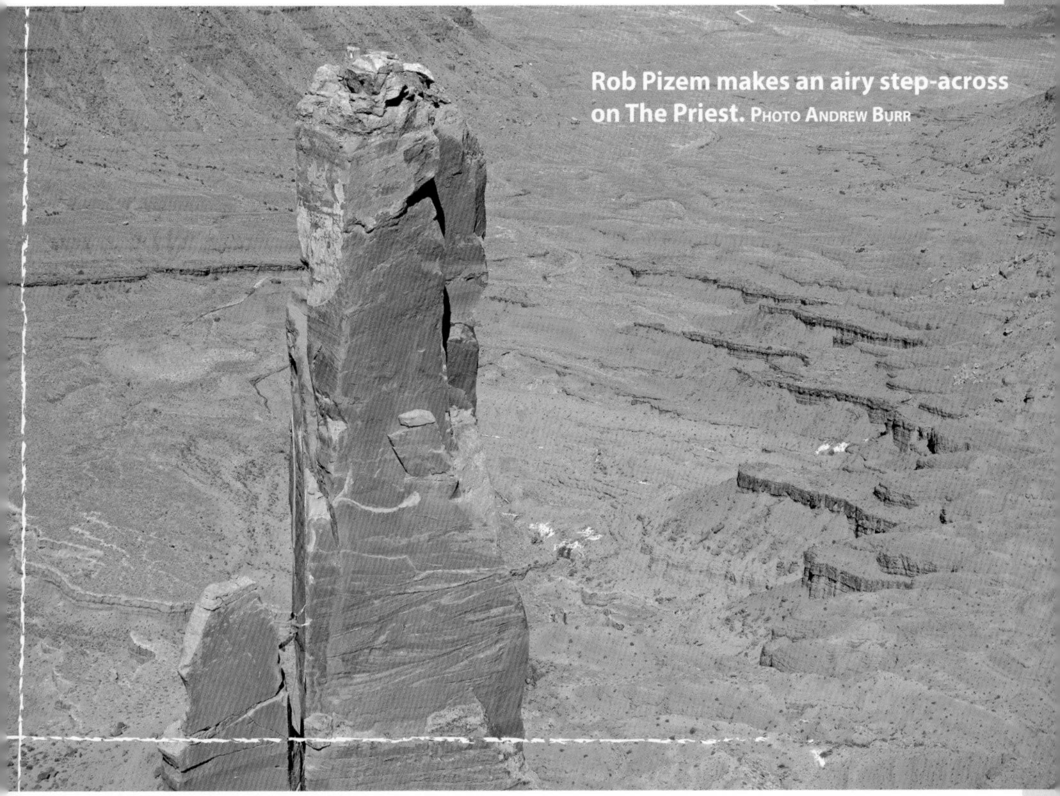

Rob Pizem makes an airy step-across on The Priest. Photo Andrew Burr

Castleton Tower

1. Kor-Ingalls Route (III 5.9) Ultra-classic tower climb with short cruxes, good rock, and a sunny exposure. It follows left-facing corners up the south face. Begin on the ridge below the face. To start, climb easy rock (4th class) to a ledge. **Pitch 1:** Climb a crack (5.5) up a corner or a squeeze chimney to the left (5.7) to another chimney (5.4). Belay on a ledge at a 2-bolt anchor. 140 feet. **Pitch 2:** Start up two parallel cracks, then commit to the right crack and jam (5.8+) up a left-facing corner to a ledge with 3 bolts. 100 feet. **Pitch 3:** Work up an awkward off-width crack and chimney in a left-facing dihedral (5.9) to a ledge. 100 feet. The off-width section can be laybacked. Look for TCU placements in the off-width. **Pitch 4:** Chimney behind the flake before exiting left on face moves (5.7) to the summit. 70 feet. **Descent:** Make four rappels down the route or preferably two 200-foot double-rope rappels or four 100-foot rappels down the *North Face.* South face rappels: **Rappel 1:** 70-foot rappel from summit bolts to ledge. **Rappel 2:** Two-rope rappel 100 feet down crux dihedral to ledge. **Rappel 3:** Two-rope rappel 100 feet to first belay ledge. **Rappel 4:** Two-rope rappel 140 feet to base of route. **Rack:** Medium and large Stoppers, TCUs, two sets of Friends to #3.5 or Camalots to #3, and slings.

2. North Chimney (III 5.8+) Excellent, popular, and fun—Castleton's easiest route. Begin on the far left side of the north face. Reach the start by hiking to the north side of the tower and scrambling up from the saddle between Castleton and The Rectory to a ledge below the north face. Go left on the ledge to the base of the route. **Pitch 1:** Jam sustained, vertical hand cracks (5.8/5.9) to a crux bulge at 130 feet. Belay 10 feet higher at a stance with two bolts. **Pitch 2:** Jam an off-width crack (5.8+), then climb over chockstones and up cracks in a moderate chimney. Continue to a belay ledge (hand-size cams). 135 feet. **Pitch 3:** Jam a hand crack, then stem up a chimney (5.8) to a notch (step across chimney into notch) between the main tower and a large flake and belay. **Pitch 4:** Join the *Kor-Ingalls Route* and face climb (5.7) up left for

Moab climber Steph Davis free-soloed the *North Face* of Castleton Tower in April 2008 and then BASE-jumped off the summit. After reaching the top, she checked the wind and realized that conditions were perfect. Steph jumped off the southwest corner of the tower "on a speedy descent—two seconds of free-fall, a minute under the canopy, and five minutes back to the car." That's got to beat rappelling and hiking down!

Castleton Tower

40 feet to the summit. **Descent:** Rappel the *North Face* with three double-rope rappels or rappel *Kor-Ingalls* with four rappels. **Rack:** Two sets of Friends with extra #3s and #3.5s or equivalent Camalots, a set of TCUs, and lots of runners. A #4 Camalot may be useful.

3. North Face (III 5.11b/c) Wild, exposed route with varied and sustained jamming. Scramble to the ledge at the base of the north face and start below a right-facing corner. **Pitch 1:** Jam a wide hand and fist crack (5.10+) up the thin right-facing corner, pass a small roof, and continue until the corner ends. Undercling up right (5.11a/b) on a hanging flake or jam a finger crack straight up, then traverse right (5.11a) to a 2-bolt belay/ rappel stance on the right. **Pitch 2:** Climb a crack (5.9) into The Pod and exit over a roof (5.10a/b hands). Work up a wide section, then continue up flakes and ledges (5.7) to a 3-bolt belay on a good ledge. **Pitch 3:** Move up right on flakes to an off-width crack (5.10). Higher, work right (5.10-) into a chimney (5.7) that emerges onto the summit. An extra belay stance is at the base of the chimney. **Descent:** Rappel the route with three double-rope rappels. It's possible to rappel with a 70-meter rope, but the first rappel from the top is a rope-stretcher—tie knots in your rope ends. **Rack:** Two sets of Friends (extra #3s and #3.5s) or Camalots (extra #2s and #3s) to #4, medium to large Stoppers, #4.5 or #5 Camalot.

Rob Pizem on the *North Face* of Castleton Tower.
PHOTO ANDREW BURR

The Rectory

The Rectory is a long, flat-topped butte north of Castleton Tower. This sky island, walled with vertical cliffs, has some fine routes including the mega-classic climb *Fine Jade*. This superb crack route on the narrow south face, first climbed by Chip Chace and Pat Ellinwood in 1984, is very popular with excellent crack climbing, good belays, and short cruxes. The route gets sun all day, making it an ideal climb during cooler weather. It can be very windy here. Watch your ropes for snags when rappelling in the wind.

Approach: Find *Fine Jade* by hiking up the Castleton trail to a junction below Castleton's north face. Go left and follow a good trail north along a narrow ridge to the route's base below The Rectory's narrow south face. Allow one and a half hours to approach the route from the parking area, three to five hours to climb, and forty-five minutes to rappel.

Descent: Make three to four rappels down the route with double ropes.

4. Fine Jade (III 5.11a) Excellent route with varied crack climbing—one of Moab's best climbs. Link pitches 2 and 3 together for faster climbing. To start, scramble atop a pedestal (5.2) below the route. **Pitch 1:** Jam an off-width/fist crack up and over a bulge (5.10d). A strenuous thin hand crack up right leads to a small roof. Pull past the roof to a short wide section. Finish up a hand crack (5.10) to a final finger crack (5.10+). Belay from bolts on a ledge. **Pitch 2:** Jam over a bulge to a finger crack (5.10), then step right to a wide section. Jam a hand then finger crack to a ledge with a 3-bolt anchor. **Pitch 3:** Step right and jam thin cracks to a horizontal break. Jam a sustained finger crack (5.11a) to a pod. Jam the finger and hand crack up left over a couple bulges to a 2-bolt anchor on a ledge. **Pitch 4:** Climb corners and ledges up right on loose sandy rock, then back left (5.9) to a good ledge with a 2-bolt anchor. **Pitch 5:** Two ways to go. For the regular finish, climb a short corner and hand traverse left (5.7) to an off-width crack in a dihedral. Climb the crack, then traverse left under a roof (5.9+) to the summit. Place lots of slings to avoid rope drag, or break it into two pitches. The direct finish climbs the corner, then face climbs (5.11a) past four bolts to the summit. **Descent:** Three rappels down the route. Watch for loose rocks. **Rappel 1:** 75-foot rappel to a 2-bolt anchor on the final belay ledge. **Rappel 2:** Two-rope rappel down to first belay stance. **Rappel 3:** Two-rope rappel to the ground. **Rack:** Two sets of Friends to #3.5 or Camalots to #3, set of TCUs, medium and large Stoppers, extra slings, and two ropes.

The Rectory

3 rappels down route
.9+
.11a
.7
.9
.11a fingers
.10
.10+
fingers
.10
.10d
4

The Priest

The Priest is a spectacular 330-foot-high pinnacle sitting at the north end of The Rectory, north of Castleton Tower. From a distance, particularly from the northeast, the tower looks like a priest. The classic *Honeymoon Chimney* offers excellent climbing with a mandatory off-width crack, a wide chimney, a wild step-across, and a small airy summit. The Priest is climbed less than Castleton and Sister Superior since it requires more commitment, so don't worry about queuing up at the base.

Approach: To reach The Priest, drive up Castle Valley Road and park at the Castleton Tower trailhead. Follow the trail to a junction on scree slopes north of Castleton's north face. Go left and hike north on a good trail along a ridge to The Rectory. Continue hiking below its west face to the base of The Priest. Allow one and a half hours to hike from car to cliff.

5. Honeymoon Chimney (III 5.11b or 5.9 A0) Excellent, exposed, and wild climb up the west face. Begin by scrambling north along a broad ledge below the face to the base of a chimney. **Pitch 1:** Climb an off-width crack with arm bars or laybacks on the left side of a large flake below the chimney. A drilled angle and quarter-inch bolt protect the moves. Continue up an unprotected off-width (5.10) for 40 feet to a wedged chockstone with slings. Enter the squeeze chimney above and tunnel upwards (5.8) to a flat belay ledge inside. 120 feet. **Pitch 2:** Follow the back-and-foot chimney (5.6) another 70 feet to a belay ledge with a 2-bolt belay/rappel anchor on the west face. A drilled angle and a few cam placements protect the chimney. **Pitch 3:** Work up the widening chimney, eventually stemming between the main tower and a subsidiary summit. Clip up a bolt ladder, then step onto the main tower and face climb (5.11b or A0) an arête to a narrow ledge with loose blocks. Place a cam to protect your second, then climb a corner up left (5.7) to a 2-bolt belay stance. 80 feet. **Pitch 4:** Work up left around a corner before finishing up a shallow left-facing corner (5.8) to the summit. 70 feet. A direct finish jams a thin crack (5.11d) up the calcite headwall above the belay. **Descent:** Make three double-rope rappels (with 165-foot ropes) to the ground. **Rappel 1:** 150 feet from summit to 2-bolt anchors atop pitch 2. **Rappel 2:** 70 feet down chimney to a ledge with rappel anchors behind the pitch 1 belay. **Rappel 3:** 130 feet down the chimney on the east side of the tower to the ground. If you rappel to the east side, it's easier to pull your ropes. It can be rappelled with two 200-foot (60-meter) ropes but the pull is tough. **Rack:** Sets of Stoppers and TCUs, one or two sets of Camalots to #3, extra slings, and two ropes. Don't bring Big Bros or big cams.

The Priest

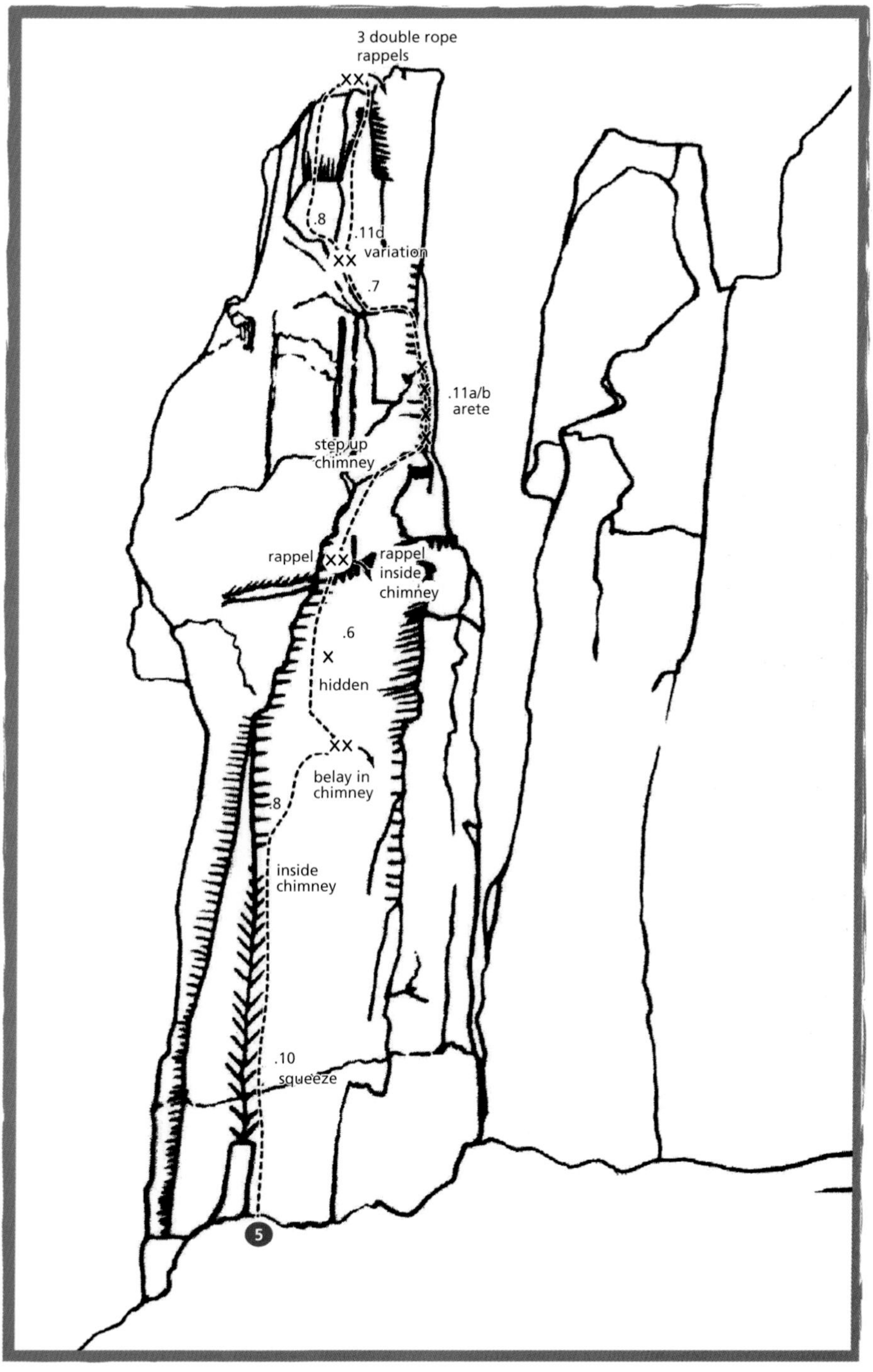

3 double rope rappels
.8
.11d
variation
.7
.11a/b
arete
step up
chimney
rappel
rappel
inside
chimney
.6
hidden
belay in
chimney
.8
inside
chimney
.10
squeeze
5

Sister Superior

Sister Superior

Sister Superior is the tallest pinnacle of a tower group perched on a ridge a couple miles north of The Priest and The Rectory. The main towers, from south to north, are Sister Superior, North Sister, Chimney Spire, and Baby Sister. *Jah Man,* up the southwest face of 330-foot-high Sister Superior, is simply one of Moab's best tower routes with short pitches, short cruxes, and great crack climbing. The route is perfect on cool days since it gets a full hit of sun. It's also very popular, especially on spring and autumn weekends. Allow a couple hours to hike to the tower, two to three hours to climb it, and an hour to rappel off.

Approach: To reach Sister Superior, continue driving east on UT 128 past Castle Valley Road and Parriott Mesa, south of the highway. After a mile, locate a track that goes right (south) up Ida Gulch just before a bridge. Walk or drive the rough road for about 2 miles. This one-lane road follows the wash and may be muddy, washed out, or impassable. Don't drive it after rain, snow, or if the weather is threatening. There are places to turn around along the road so you can stop and park. Most four-wheel-drive vehicles can make it to a boulder choke before parking.

Look for a large cairn, which marks the start of the access trail, on the left where the road bends right in the wash. Follow the trail up talus slopes to the tower. If it's possible to drive to the trailhead, allow an hour of hiking. If the road is impassable, allow two hours to hike from the highway to the tower base.

6. Jah Man (III 5.10+) Excellent and recommended. **Pitch 1:** Face climb (5.9 move) up right 20 feet and traverse right to the base of an obvious chimney (optional belay). Squeeze (5.8+) up the chimney (the Sister Squeeze) in the left-facing dihedral to a 2-bolt belay ledge. Find gear inside the chimney. **Pitch 2:** Crux lead. Jam thin hand cracks up a hollow flake in a shallow left-facing corner (5.10) to an old bolt that protects a 5.10+ move left. Above, work up an easier corner (5.8+) to a 2-bolt belay ledge. **Pitch 3:** Climb up left along splitter thin hands cracks (5.10b/c) and continue to a large belay ledge with bolt anchors on the right shoulder. 100 feet. **Pitch 4:** Face climb (5.9+) to the summit past drilled angles. 30 feet. **Descent:** Four rappels down the route with a single 200-foot (60-meter) rope. Other rappel combos are possible. **Rack:** Set of TCUs or Aliens; selection of Stoppers; Camalots: two to three #.5s, four to six #.75s, three to four #1s, two to three #2s and #3s or double sets of Friends with three to four #1.5s, four to five #2s, and one #3 and #3.5; slings; and a 200-foot (60-meter) rope.

Fisher Towers

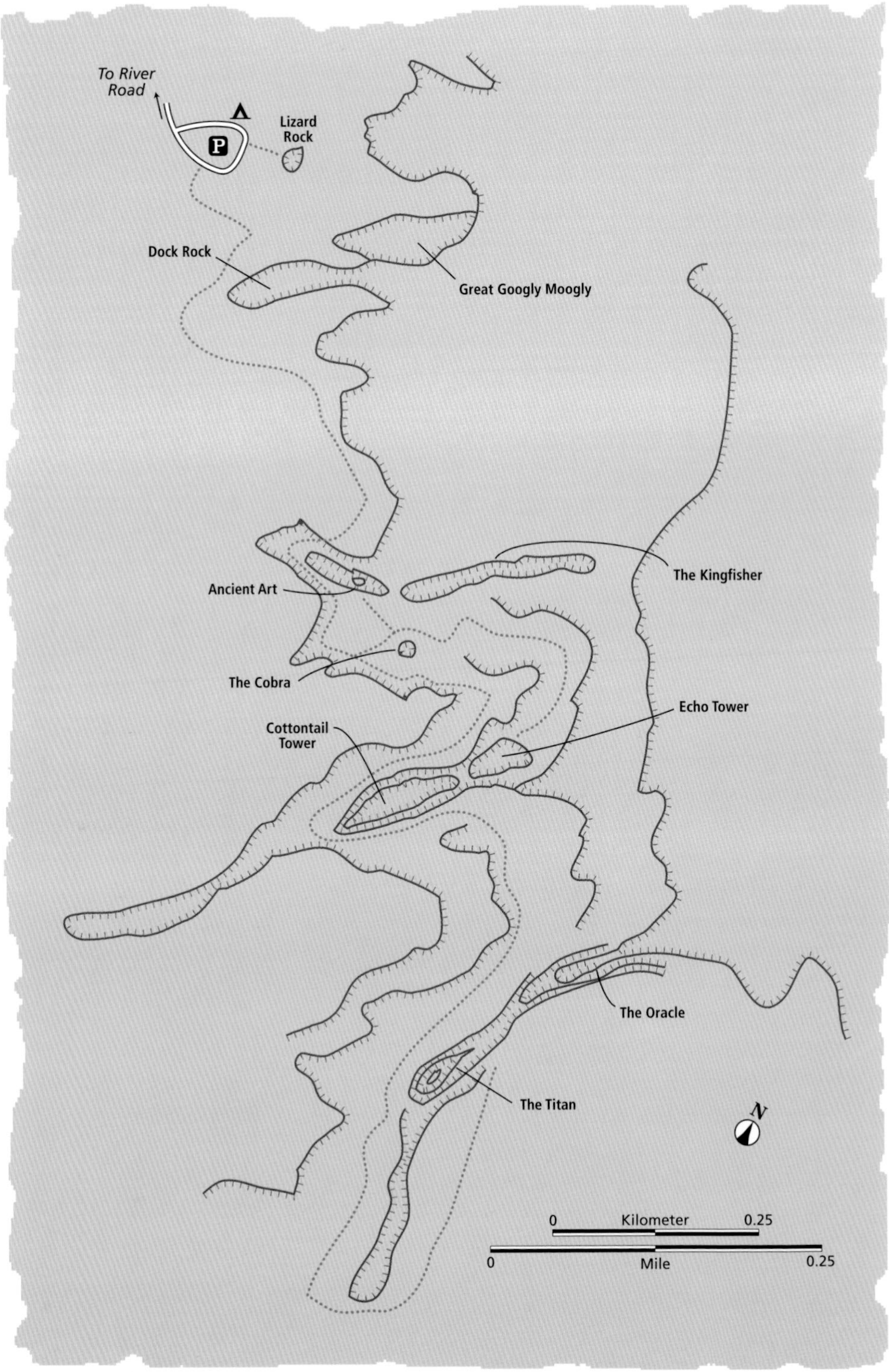

To River Road
Lizard Rock
Dock Rock
Great Googly Moogly
Ancient Art
The Kingfisher
The Cobra
Echo Tower
Cottontail Tower
The Oracle
The Titan
N
0
Kilometer
0.25
0
Mile
0.25

8.

Fisher Towers

The Fisher Towers, one of the canyon country's most bizarre landscapes, is a red maze of towering pinnacles, fins, minarets, gargoyles, and strangely shaped rock formations east of Moab. The soaring towers, draped with mud curtains, are composed of Cutler sandstone, a coarse conglomerate that is usually more solid than it looks.

The Fishers offer rock climbers lots of big aid routes up the soaring spires. The tallest is the 900-foot-high Titan. The other tall towers are Cottontail Tower, The Oracle, Echo Tower, and The Kingfisher. These towers are beyond the scope of this book and are not the best climbs except to intrepid climbers who like pounding pitons in dried mud, hanging belays, and bivouacs shared with biting cone nose bugs (yes, they're as nasty as they sound!), and who have a few days to kill.

Instead check out Ancient Art, one of the best and most popular climbs in the Moab area. Ancient Art offers decent climbing and the absolute coolest summit of any desert tower. The other best climbs are small towers that are easily accessible from the Fisher Towers parking lot. A few campsites are at the Fisher Towers trailhead. Bring water and pack out your trash.

Getting there: See the Castle Valley Towers map in chapter 7. Drive north from Moab on US 191 and just before the Colorado River Bridge, turn right (east) onto UT 128, River Road. Follow this paved highway for almost 23 miles to a turnoff marked FISHER TOWERS. Turn right (south) and follow a dirt road southeast for another 2 miles to a parking area on the north side of the towers (GPS N 38.43.489 / W 109.18.531). To reach the climbs, follow a 2.2-mile hiking trail that

The Fisher Towers are composed of the Cutler Formation—a 10,000-foot-thick layer of sandstone, mudstone, and conglomerate deposited during the Permian Age between 300 million and 250 million years ago. Fast flowing rivers and streams deposited the red rock along the western flank of Uncompahgria, an ancient mountain range to the east. Pale Moenkopi sandstone, dating to 230 million years ago, caps the Cutler Formation and retards its erosion.

begins at the parking lot and winds through the towers to a viewpoint southwest of The Titan or use climber trails that radiate out from the parking area to nearby formations.

Lizard Rock

Lizard Rock, an obvious 65-foot-high pinnacle, stands alone on the edge of a wash east of the parking lot. Lizard Rock is a great introduction to the wild world of Fisher Towers climbing with runout moves, some mud, and a cool summit. The spire's sandstone is surprisingly solid. These routes are not good for toproping because the summit anchors are set back from the edge. Approach time from car to climb is one minute.

1. Entry Fee (5.9- R) Begin on the southwest side (GPS N 38.43.505 / W 109.18.467). Climb past a flake (sling for pro) to a horizontal flake-crack. Place a #4 Camalot behind the flake to protect the crux. Stand on the flake and move up right (5.9-) to a sloping shelf and easier rock on the south side. Mantle onto the summit. **Descent:** Rappel 65 feet. **Rack:** Long runner and #4 Camalot.

2. Entry Lizards (5.9- R) The spire's best climb and a combo of *Entry Fee* and *Leaping Lizards.* Climb the first part of *Entry Fee* to the right traverse, then climb straight up to the summit on unprotected rock. A hidden hole is a good handhold for the summit mantle. **Descent:** Rappel 65 feet. **Rack:** #4 Camalot and runners.

3. Leaping Lizards (5.10 R) A direct line up the west face. Good but runout route. Follow a thin crack to a band of pebbles. Climb into a shallow corner and continue up rounded jugs to the summit. **Descent:** Rappel 65 feet. **Rack:** Stoppers, TCUs, and quickdraws.

Brian Shelton belays Bill Springer on Lizard Rock.

Lizard Rock

Dock Rock

Dock Rock is the low formation south of the parking lot. It's easy to climb and has good views of the Fisher Towers. Hike south for a few minutes from the parking area to the northwest corner of the rock.

4. Impish (5.5) No topo. Short and easy. Lots of ways to go when you climb—pick the best line. Climb broken cracks to a big ledge. Continue up right, passing a 2-bolt anchor, to the south side of the formation. Pick a line and climb to the summit. **Descent:** Rappel from bolt anchors. You may need to replace the webbing. **Rack:** Camalots to #3, slings, and quickdraws.

Great Googly Moogly

The Great Googly Moogly (gotta love that name!) is a 120-foot-high tower/fin with several summits. The tower, rising above a narrow canyon and bench east of Dock Rock, is southeast of the parking area. The route offers decent free climbing for the Fishers.

Approach: From the parking area, hike south on social trails toward Dock Rock, the obvious long lower formation directly south. Follow a path left (east) along a ridgeline that divides two drainages. Keep right and cross the right-hand canyon, then follow a trail along a flat bench west to the tower. The route, on the shady north side, offers fun but strenuous crack climbing along with some mud and a good scare factor.

"Great googly moogly," an expression of surprise, originated with Chicago blues singer Howlin' Wolf in his song "Going Down Slow." Later Frank Zappa popularized the phrase in his 1973 song "Nanook Rubs It."

5. Great Googly Moogly (5.10+) Begin below a crack system on the left side of the north face (GPS N 38.43.441 / W 109.18.360). Climb a dirty seam to a stance, then squirm up an off-width/fist crack in a short left-facing corner. Continue up right along a scary mud and rock ramp to the base of a crack. Thrutch up the overhanging off-width crack (5.10+) to a rest, then finish up a wider and easier crack to a 2-bolt anchor on a ledge. Scramble to the summit. **Descent:** Rappel 110 feet. **Rack:** Medium and large Stoppers, set of TCUs, single Camalots from #.5 to #2, double #3 and #4 Camalots, and one #5 Camalot.

Great Googly Moogly

Ancient Art

Ancient Art, the first major formation encountered on the trail to the main Fisher Towers area, is a grotesque three-summited tower. An excellent moderate route ascends to a balanced corkscrew and the most unique and wildest summit in Utah canyon country. The classic *Stolen Chimney* route ascends the south side of the tower. Expect interesting climbing, good protection, some mud and choss, and lots of exposure. This is not a beginner route.

Approach: From the parking lot at the end of the road, follow the Fisher Towers trail south through a series of shallow canyons and directly below Ancient Art's intimidating southwest face. Continue past the face to a ridge above a canyon (GPS N 38.72.134 / W 109.30.390). Hike left up a good trail that passes beneath the obvious small spire called The Cobra. Continue up to the right and then traverse left across a bench to the broken rock below a prominent chimney on Ancient Art's south face (GPS N 38.72.123 / W 109.30.330).

> Jimmie Dunn has soloed Ancient Art over 100 times. "I've done it a lot," he says. "I never free-solo though. I pull on the bolts with a quickdraw so I'm half-climbing and my feet are on the rock. I climb pretty fast." Jim always climbs to the summit of the Corkscrew. "I stand on top and then sit down for a minute. It's so beautiful up there." Coming down, says Jimmie, is "super easy. I slither down the chimney in no time." When he passes other climbers on the route, he tells them, "Don't worry. I've climbed this a lot!"

6. Stolen Chimney (II 5.10+ or 5.8 A0) Begin below a chimney. **Pitch 1:** Climb straight up (5.7) using face holds and a short hand crack to the base of a groove. Pinch pebbles and cobbles (5.10 or A0) past four drilled angles to a 2-bolt ledge belay. 120 feet. **Pitch 2:** Climb the well-protected mud chimney (5.8) to a 3-bolt belay ledge on the right. **Pitch 3:** Climb onto a block and face climb up a ridge (5.10+) with three bolts to a 3-bolt belay. 40 feet. **Pitch 4:** Walk or crawl across The Sidewalk, an exposed ridge, to the Diving Board, a jutting sandstone tongue. Mantle on it (5.8), then grab good holds (5.8) to a sling anchor on the corkscrew summit (GPS N 38.72.160 / W 109.30.423). **Descent:** Three rappels. Lower from the summit and traverse back across The Sidewalk to a 3-bolt anchor. **Rappel 1:** Single-rope rappel to anchors atop pitch 2. **Rappel 2:** Single-rope rappel to anchors atop pitch 1. **Rappel 3:** Double-rope rappel to the ground. **Rack:** Set of Friends or Camalots with extra #1s and #3s, medium to large Stoppers, quickdraws, extra slings, and two ropes or a 70-meter rope.

Ancient Art

sling anchor
Diving Board
5.10 or A0
bolt ladder
5.8
chimney
5.10 or A0
bolt ladder
6

Carson's Tower

Carson's Tower is a 60-foot-high isolated spire perched on a broad ridge north of the Fisher Towers. The tower, standing alone between the Fishers and River Road, is northeast of the Fisher Towers road. It offers a short fun route to a cool summit. The hike out to the tower takes longer than the climb.

Approach: (See Castle Valley Towers map in chapter 7.) Locate the tower from the Fisher Towers road. Park on the road's shoulder southwest of the tower and hike cross-country to it. Follow washes whenever possible and avoid stepping on cryptobiotic soil. Alternatively, park at the main parking lot and hike north from the campsites down a big wash. The route is on the south side of the formation (GPS N 38.73.534 / W 109.31.824).

7. Carson Chimney (5.7) Climb an easy chimney to a wide section. Place a #3 Camalot with a long sling and tie off a horn on the right side, then clip a couple drilled pitons. Stem across the gap and pull (5.7 move) onto the main tower. Finish up easy rock to a 2-bolt anchor below the top. Scramble onto the summit. **Descent:** Rappel to the base. **Rack:** #3 and #4.5 Camalots, extra slings, and quickdraws.

Carson's Tower

9.

Looking Glass Rock

Looking Glass Rock, an Entrada sandstone dome lying a couple miles west of US 191 south of Moab, offers a fun three-pitch route up an exposed fin to a domed summit. The highlight, however, is a spectacular 185-foot free rappel that drops out of an exposed keyhole window. The easy route, first done by local cowboys years ago, is mostly easy friction climbing protected by a few bolts. The summit views are marvelous, with the snowcapped La Sal Mountains looming to the northeast and the Henry and Abajo Mountains to the west and southwest.

The *East Rib* route is easy but exposed. It's well protected and has 2-bolt anchors for belaying. The free rappel, however, is not for beginners. It's tricky to start from the small window, and once you get down about 8 feet, it's completely free to the ground. If your climbing partner is a novice or freaked out, consider lowering them down. Avoid climbing the route in windy conditions or for a day or two after rain or snow. Give the rock a chance to dry out and it will be less sandy.

Getting there: (See overview map with table of contents.) Drive south from Moab on US 191 for 20 miles. At La Sal Junction, the junction of US 191 and UT 46, continue 0.6 mile south on US 191 and turn west onto Looking Glass Road (San Juan County Road 131). Drive 1.8 miles on the sandy road to Looking Glass Rock, a large humped dome to the left. Turn onto a spur road and drive 0.1 mile to a parking area and turnaround on the west side of the rock (GPS N 38.27 .532 / W 109.40.661). There is a good primitive campsite and a spot for viewing Looking Glass Arch.

Looking Glass Arch was named, according to Eric Bjørnstad in *Desert Rock IV,* in 1889 by John Silvery "because the sun shining through the opening creates an image on the wall of the deep cave, which reminded him of that created by a mirror or looking glass." The arch, a landmark on the Old Spanish Trail, is 34 feet high and 43 feet wide. The route described here was first climbed by local cowboys—yeehaw!

Dennis Jump makes a spectacular free rappel off Looking Glass Rock.

To reach the base of the route, hike around the north side of the dome on slabs and sand to the base of the long obvious east ridge. Step across a fence at the toe of the ridge. Start the route on a slab below a short corner on the southeast side of the ridge (GPS N 38.27.517 / W 109.40.358).

1. East Rib (5.4) Begin just left of the toe of the ridge below a short corner. **Pitch 1:** Climb the corner (5.4) to a flat ledge with a bolt. Climb easily to a bolt in a white rock band and continue to a third bolt, then finish up a short crack to a nice belay ledge with a 2-bolt anchor. 145 feet. **Pitch 2:** Climb past three bolts on the narrow ridge, passing a smearing crux (5.4) above the second bolt, to a 2-bolt anchor at a good stance. 130 feet. **Pitch 3:** Scramble up the easy ridge to the left (4th class) past a bolt to a 2-bolt anchor on flat sandstone. 140 feet. Unrope and walk west along a wide terrace to three drilled pitons and two bolts. Leave your ropes here and scramble to the spacious summit. **Descent:** From the five pitons/bolts, look into a gap with a keyhole and locate a 4-bolt rappel anchor above the gaping hole. Belay down an easy but exposed rib above the keyhole to the anchors. Make a 185-foot free rappel from the keyhole window to the ground on the south side of the formation and east of Looking Glass Arch. **Rack:** Six quickdraws, several long slings, and two 200-foot (60-meter) ropes. Shorter ropes will not work!

Looking Glass Rock

Canyonlands—Washer Woman

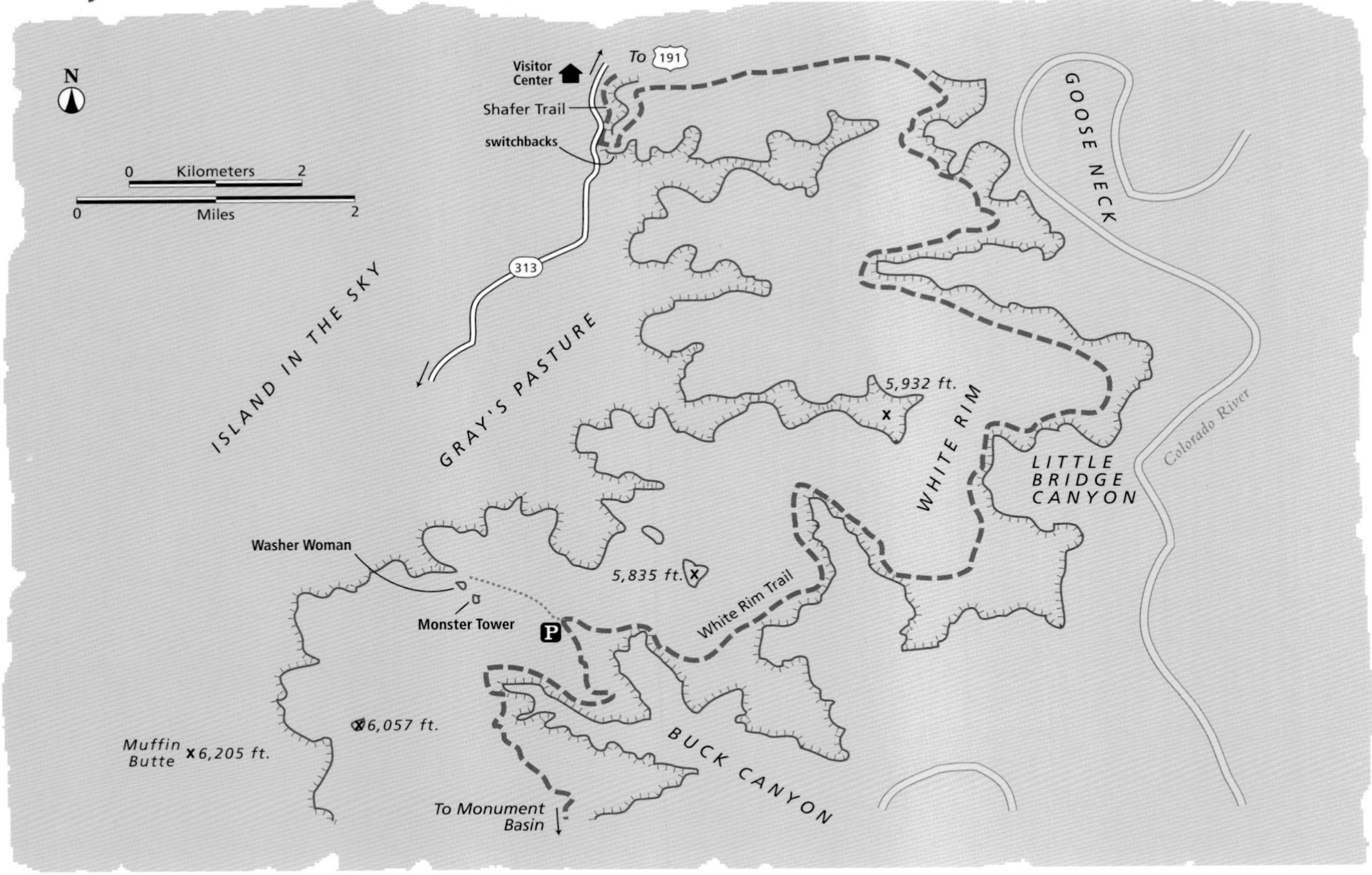

10. Canyonlands National Park

The Island in the Sky dominates the northern part of 337,570-acre Canyonlands National Park. The Island, a 6,000-foot-high mesa lined with Wingate sandstone cliffs, rises above the Colorado River on the east and the Green River on the west. Deep canyons, isolated buttes, and tall towers cut into the Island's cliffs. This sector of Canyonlands offers climbers some of the area's best tower adventures, with spectacular routes ascending soaring faces.

The towers, including the two towers described here—Moses and Washer Woman, are reached by rough dirt roads and jeep tracks but yield some of Moab's best adventure climbs. Other Island in the Sky towers include Zeus, Aphrodite, Charlie Horse Needle, The Witch, Candlestick Tower, Monster Tower, and Standing Rock.

Danger lurks everywhere on the Island in the Sky towers, with fractured rock and loose blocks on many ledges or wedged in cracks and chimneys. Wear a helmet, climb cautiously on loose sections, and protect your belayer from rockfall. Carry lots of water, especially on hot days. A gallon a day per person is not too much. Approaches to the towers are long and time-consuming. Plan on plenty of time to drive to the trailheads, approach the towers, do the routes, and drive back to Moab. Remember that you can't camp or bivouac at the towers without a backcountry permit. Also carry a headlamp in case the climb takes too long, your ropes stick on a rappel, or you have to hike back at night.

Camping is allowed along the White Rim Trail only at designated sites, most of which are booked in advance by mountain bikers. Backcountry permits, available without reservations, allow camping near many climbing sites. They're available at the Island in the Sky ranger station or by mail from park headquarters. Backcountry camping must be at least a mile from the road. Primitive camping is allowed outside the park boundary.

Descent from the towers is by rappelling. The rappel stations and anchors are usually obvious. Check all webbing on anchors and replace if it's brittle or faded. Tie knots in rope ends to avoid rappelling off them. Be careful not to dislodge rocks when rappelling or pulling your ropes; climbers may be below. It's best to have double ropes for all rappels unless you're absolutely sure a doubled single rope will reach.

Canyonlands National Park has several rock climbing regulations that are enforced. Know the rules and follow them to ensure continued access to the park's towers and cliffs. No permit is required for rock climbing, but a permit is required for all backcountry camping and bivouacking. Climbing in the park is limited to free climbing and hammerless, clean-aid climbing. The placement of fixed hardware, including bolts, drilled pitons, nuts, and other fixed gear as well as the placement of any gear with a hammer is prohibited. The only exception is in emergency situations. Check at the visitor center at Island in the Sky for permits and updated information on regulations and road conditions.

Getting there: The Island in the Sky and Canyonlands National Park are reached by driving northeast from Moab on US 191 for 10 miles or 22 miles southeast from I-70. Turn south on UT 313 and drive 22 miles to the Canyonlands ranger station and the start of the Shafer Trail. To reach Moses and Taylor Canyon, turn right or west from UT 313 after driving 12 miles on the gravel Mineral Canyon Road.

Washer Woman

Washer Woman is a spectacular finlike tower perched on a high ridge next to Monster Tower on the east side of the Island in the Sky. Washer Woman, split by a huge arch, resembles a woman leaning over an old-fashioned washtub when viewed from a distance. The remote tower offers three routes, but *In Search of Suds* is simply one of the best tower climbs in the Moab region. Expect excellent crack climbing, an interesting face pitch to the summit, a wild free rappel down the arch, and great views across the White Rim and Colorado River to the La Sal Mountains.

Approach: Washer Woman is west of the White Rim Trail, a rough 98-mile track that circles around the east side of the Island in the Sky. The easiest approach is to drive northwest

Rick Horn, John Horn, and Pete Carmen climbed Washer Woman in the spring of 1967. The party used wooden wedges in big cracks and an ice piton hammered into rotten rock. The tower wasn't repeated until 1982 when Charlie Fowler and Glenn Randall established *In Search of Suds*.

from Moab on US 191 for 10 miles to UT 313. Turn left (south) on UT 313 and drive 22 miles to the Island in the Sky ranger station and visitor center. Just past the station, turn left onto the Shafer Trail, a winding dirt road that descends 1,200 feet and 4 miles down switchbacks to the White Rim Trail. Do not attempt this road if it's wet, snowy, or icy. A four-wheel-drive vehicle is advised for both the Shafer and White Rim Trails.

The junction of the Shafer and White Rim Trails is also reached from Moab by driving north on US 191 a couple miles to UT 279. Turn left onto UT 279 (Potash Road) and follow the paved highway past Wall Street to the Potash Mine. Continue south on a rough dirt road for 14.5 miles to the Shafer Trail–White Rim Trail junction. This is a better route during bad weather or if Shafer Trail is wet or icy. This road can be rough or washed out after thunderstorms.

From the junction of the Shafer and White Rim Trails, drive the White Rim Trail south for 13 miles to the head of Buck Canyon. The drive takes a couple hours to reach the obvious tower. Park on slickrock beside the road. Hike up Buck Canyon, keeping left. Look for a climber's path that breaks left and scrambles up steep talus slopes toward Washer Woman and Monster Tower.

To reach Washer Woman and the described route, you have two choices. Hike toward a notch between Washer Woman and Monster Tower. In broken rock, find a crack system left of Washer Woman and climb a 75-foot crack (5.6) to the notch. Scramble over to the route's base. Or scramble around the base of Monster Tower to the southwest face of Washer Woman. The route begins below an obvious crack system and the ledge from the notch on the right side of the face.

1. In Search of Suds (III 5.10+) The line follows a crack system up the right side of the southwest face before traversing along a narrow ridge to the summit. Begin on the right side of the southwest face left of a prominent ridge. This makes the first pitch into a 150-foot lead. Otherwise, follow a ledge system from the notch between Washer Woman and Monster Tower to a belay below the crack system. This description begins there. **Pitch 1:** Jam a fist crack (5.9+) and off-width crack in the back of a chimney to a bolted belay stance below a small window that penetrates the tower, called Eye of the Needle. Watch for loose rock. 85 feet. **Pitch 2:** Jam a hand crack (5.9-) left of the Eye to an easier crack (5.7). Continue up a flared chimney past a bulge, then make an awkward escape left onto a ledge with a 3-bolt anchor below a roof. 90 feet. **Pitch 3:** Jam a hand and fist crack (5.10) through the roof, then make tough moves (5.10+) over a bulge. Climb cracks (5.9) to the ridgeline and a gear belay. 70 feet. **Pitch 4:** Traverse along the easy but

Washer Woman

airy ridge (5.6) to a belay below a headwall. 70 feet. **Pitch 5:** Face climb up a headwall (5.9) over the large arch. Pro is old pins. Belay from bolts on a ledge below the final step. **Pitch 6:** Face climb over rotten rock bands (5.9 R) to a bolt ladder on a smooth face. Follow the hard-to-clip bolts (5.10 or C1) to a great summit. **Descent:** Three or four double-rope rappels down the original route. Dangerous and loose descent. Be careful of rockfall when pulling the rope! **Rappel 1:** Rappel back to the belay atop the arch. **Rappel 2:** Make a scary, exposed free rappel down the arch from poorly positioned anchors to anchors on a good ledge at its base. Hardest part is getting over the top edge. **Rappel 3:** Rappel to the ground with double 200-foot ropes or rappel to bolt anchors on a ledge. **Rappel 4:** Rappel to the ground. **Rack:** Two sets of Friends or Camalots with four #3s, sets of TCUs and Stoppers, and two ropes.

Moab rock collector Lin Ottinger's mother named Moses in the 1950s when she exclaimed, "Look Lin, that pinnacle looks like Moses!" Earlier, uranium prospectors called it Monkey Rock. Eric Bjørnstad and Fred Beckey were the first climbers to view Moses, when Ottinger took the pair on a reconnaissance flight over Taylor Canyon in 1970. They returned on October 21, 1972, with Jim Galvin, Tom Nephew, and Gregory Markov to climb the *North Face* for the tower's first ascent, which took five days. That route, free-climbed by Charlie Fowler and Chip Chace in 1981, is now called *Pale Fire.*

Moses

Taylor Canyon, on the north boundary of Canyonlands National Park, is a deep cliff-lined canyon that twists west from the top of the Island in the Sky to the Green River on the west side of the park. Some of Utah's most famous sandstone skyscrapers—Moses, Zeus, and Aphrodite—hide in upper Taylor Canyon.

Moses, a 500-foot-high freestanding tower, is simply one of the best and most rewarding tower climbs. *The Primrose Dihedrals,* which ascends the southeast face, is the best climb on Moses and one of the best hard routes in the desert. It offers compact sandstone, varied jamming, lots of exposures, short boulder-problem cruxes, and a small airy summit. Plan on a full day to climb the tower and rappel off.

Approach: Drive northwest from Moab on US 191 for 10 miles to a left (south) turn onto UT 313, which heads to Dead Horse Point and Island in the Sky. Drive the paved highway for 12

Canyonlands—Moses

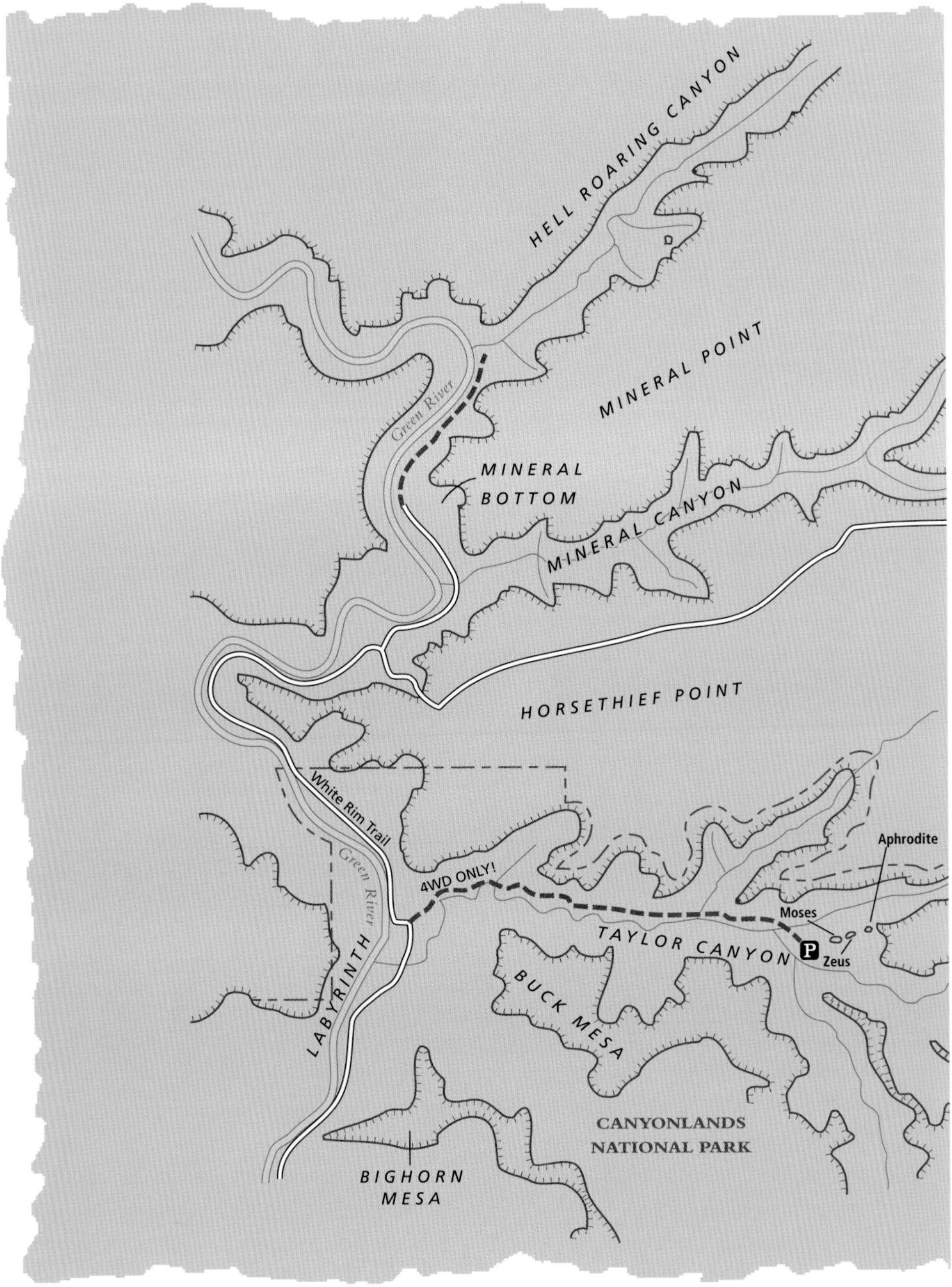

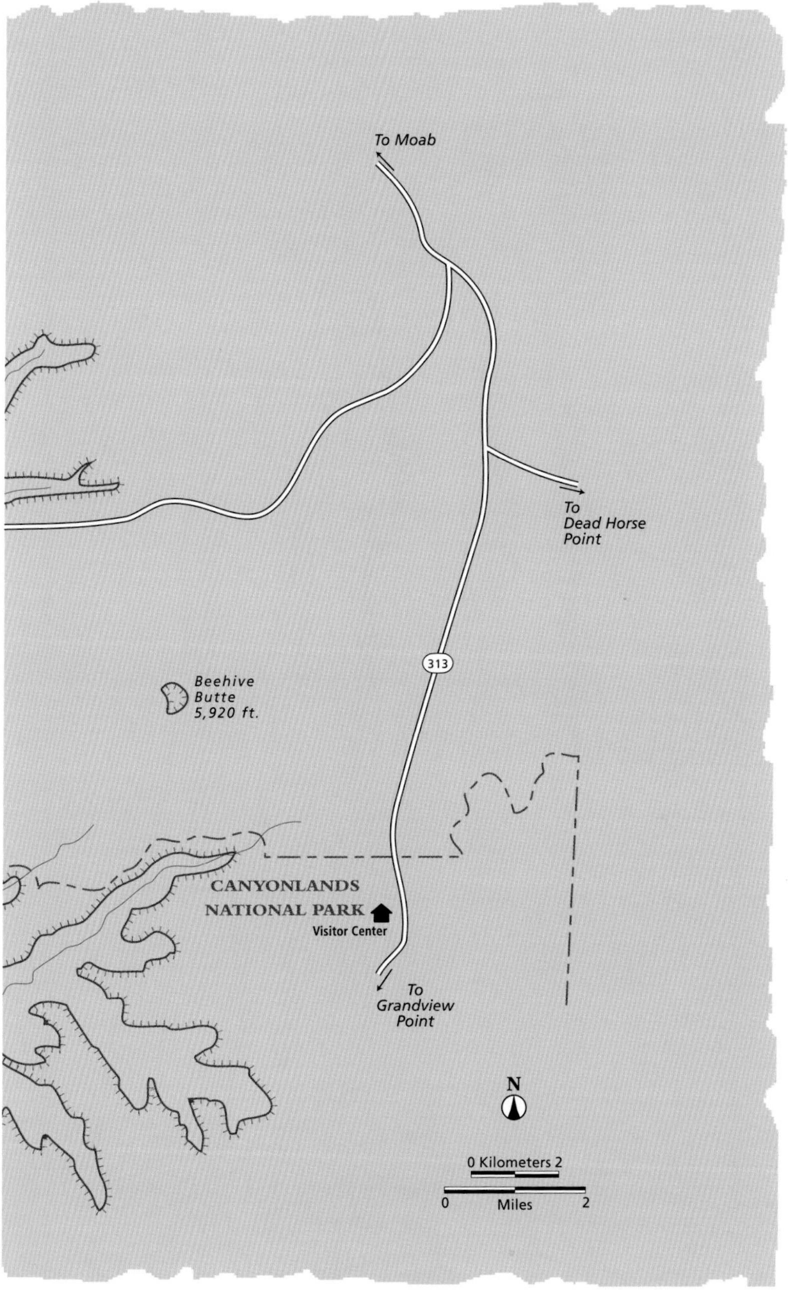
To Moab
To Dead Horse Point
313
Beehive Butte 5,920 ft.
CANYONLANDS NATIONAL PARK
Visitor Center
To Grandview Point
N
0 Kilometers 2
0 Miles 2

Moses

5 rappels down face
.8
.8
hidden chimney
The Ear
.11b
LB
.9
loose
.10
scary
sloping ledge
.10-
.10b
.10 roof
step down approach notch from north side
fingers
.8
.11d
slot
2

miles to a right turn signed HORSETHIEF TRAIL. Follow this dirt road across the mesa to the canyon rim. Descend the rough and narrow Horsethief Trail road down steep switchbacks to the canyon floor and the Green River. A high-clearance vehicle is advised. It's dangerous and slick when wet or icy. Use caution.

At Horsethief Bottom on the canyon floor, turn left (south) and follow the White Rim Trail for 0.8 mile to the Canyonlands National Park boundary. Continue south a couple miles to a well-marked left turn up Taylor Canyon. Follow the rough road (four-wheel-drive, high-clearance, tire pump, and shovel recommended) for almost 5 miles to the base of Moses. The track is alternately sandy and rocky. It is impassable after rain. Road conditions vary from year to year. It may be passable all or partway with a two-wheel-drive vehicle. Check at the Island in the Sky ranger station for conditions and details.

2. Primrose Dihedrals (III 5.11d) Best climb on the desert's proudest tower. Begin below a crack system on the right side of the southeast face. **Pitch 1:** Climb broken rock bands to an inverted chimney slot (5.11d). Continue up broken rock to a ledge with two bolts. 80 feet. Avoid this pitch by approaching from the north to the notch east of Moses. Step down (5.8) and traverse left to the ledge. **Pitch 2:** Jam an obvious crack in a corner. Fingers (5.10-) to hands (5.10) lead over a roof, then pass a fixed pin to a layback (5.10-). Belay from bolts in an alcove. **Pitch 3:** Clip a fixed piton and move down left (5.8) to a leftward traverse. Climb cracks and stacked flakes (5.10-) to a sloping ledge with two bolts. **Pitch 4:** Jam a crack up a right-facing dihedral, then climb a large spike into a corner. Jam and layback (5.10) to a roof. Continue above up a fist and off-width crack to a semi-hanging belay stance. **Pitch 5:** Climb a dihedral past loose, stacked blocks (5.9) to a belay below The Ear, an overhanging flake. **Pitch 6:** Scary and airy. Layback or off-width up an 8-inch overhanging crack (5.11b) using a bolt ladder for pro. Higher, squeeze into a crack and end on a ledge with bolts. **Pitch 7:** Work up left in a chimney (5.8) to a shoulder, then face climb (5.8) to the summit. **Descent:** Make four to five double-rope rappels down *Pale Fire* on the north face. Some are scary because they have hanging stations. Or rappel the *South Directissema Route* right of *Primrose* with four or five double-rope rappels. **Rack:** Two sets of Friends with three #1.5s, three #3s, and three #3.5s (extra #1 to #2 Friends and a 5-inch piece are also useful); sets of TCUs and Stoppers; slings; and two ropes.

Appendix: Additional Information

Climbing Equipment

Gearheads Outdoor Store
471 South Main St.
Moab, UT 84532
(888) 740-4327

Pagan Mountaineering
59 S. Main St., #2
Moab, Utah 84532
(435) 259-1117
www.climbmoab.com
www.paganclimber.com

Climbing Guides

Front Range Climbing Company (Climbing Guides)
722 N. 31st St.
Colorado Springs, CO
(866) 572-3722
www.frontrangeclimbing.com

Jackson Hole Mountain Guides (Climbing Guides)
P.O. Box 7477
Jackson, WY 83002
(435) 260-0990 or (877) 270-6622

Moab Cliffs and Canyons (Climbing and Canyoneering Guides)
253 N. Main St.
Moab, UT 84532
(435) 259-3317 or (877) 641-5271
www.cliffsandcanyons.com

Moab Desert Adventures (Climbing and Canyoneering Guides)
415 N. Main St.
Moab, UT 84532
(877) ROK-MOAB or (435) 260-2404
www.moabdesertadventures.com

Management Agencies

Arches National Park
P.O. Box 907
Moab, UT 84532
(435) 719-2299
www.nps.gov/arch/index.htm

Bureau of Land Management

Moab Field Office
82 E. Dogwood
Moab, Utah 84532
(435) 259-2100
www.blm.gov/ut/st/en/fo/moab.html

BLM Camping Information
www.blm.gov/ut/st/en/fo/moab/recreation/campgrounds.html

Canyonlands National Park
2282 SW Resource Blvd.
Moab, Utah 84532
(435) 719-2313
Backcountry Information
(435) 259-4351
www.nps.gov/cany/index.htm

Moab Information

Official Moab, Utah, Home Page
www.moab.net

Moab Information Site
www.moab-utah.com

Moab Official Tourist Information
www.discovermoab.com

Moab, Utah, Travel Guide
www.go-utah.com/moab

Medical Services

Allen Memorial Hospital
719 W. 400 North
Moab, UT 84532
(435) 259-7191
www.amhmoab.org

For emergencies call:
Grand County Sheriff's Office
(435) 259-8115 or 911

Grand County Search and Rescue (GCSAR)
P.O. Box 1343
Moab, UT 84532
www.gcsar.org

Index